Beginning Data Science, IoT, and AI on Single Board Computers

Core Skills and Real-World Application with the BBC micro:bit and XinaBox

Philip Meitiner
Pradeeka Seneviratne

Apress®

Beginning Data Science, IoT, and AI on Single Board Computers: Core Skills and Real-World Application with the BBC micro:bit and XinaBox

Philip Meitiner
Yorkshire, UK

Pradeeka Seneviratne
Udumulla, Mulleriyawa, Sri Lanka

ISBN-13 (pbk): 978-1-4842-5765-4
https://doi.org/10.1007/978-1-4842-5766-1

ISBN-13 (electronic): 978-1-4842-5766-1

Managing Director, Apress Media LLC: Welmoed Spahr
Acquisitions Editor: Natalie Pao
Development Editor: James Markham
Coordinating Editor: Jessica Vakili

Distributed to the book trade worldwide by Springer Science+Business Media New York, 233 Spring Street, 6th Floor, New York, NY 10013. Phone 1-800-SPRINGER, fax (201) 348-4505, e-mail orders-ny@springer-sbm.com, or visit www.springeronline.com. Apress Media, LLC is a California LLC and the sole member (owner) is Springer Science + Business Media Finance Inc (SSBM Finance Inc). SSBM Finance Inc is a **Delaware** corporation.

For information on translations, please e-mail rights@apress.com, or visit http://www. apress.com/rights-permissions.

Apress titles may be purchased in bulk for academic, corporate, or promotional use. eBook versions and licenses are also available for most titles. For more information, reference our Print and eBook Bulk Sales web page at http://www.apress.com/bulk-sales.

Any source code or other supplementary material referenced by the author in this book is available to readers on GitHub via the book's product page, located at www.apress.com/ 978-1-4842-5765-4. For more detailed information, please visit http://www.apress.com/ source-code.

Printed on acid-free paper

Table of Contents

About the Authors

Philip Meitiner graduated from the University of Kwa-Zulu Natal with a social science degree and education diploma, and began his career teaching mathematics and lecturing psychology to tertiary level disadvantaged students. After three years in education he spent a decade in market research, and still talks about being THE authority on the intricacies of the washing powder market in South Africa in the 1990s. After a brief stint as a freelance programmer, he spent the 2000s as a project manager in web design agencies until twice being made redundant during the great crash. Philip then moved into consultancy, initially software development, until he was approached by the BBC and asked to be program manager on the BBC micro:bit project. After the successful delivery of this epic project, Philip was one of the original members of the Micro:bit Educational Foundation, where he helped establish micro:bit as a global brand. He is now COO for Europe at XinaBox. This eclectic mix of careers and experience has instilled in Philip a deep understanding of what it is like to embark on a new learning journey. In addition, his experiences in teaching, market research, and IT have given him a unique mix of skills and knowledge, which are laid bare in the pages ahead.

Pradeeka Seneviratne is a graduate from the Sri Lanka Institute of Information Technology (SLIIT). He has nearly two decades of experience working on large and complex IT projects in the industrial world. Pradeeka has focused on different technologies and software in a variety of fields and roles, such as programmer, analyst, architect, and team leader. He has also authored several maker-related books, including *Beginning BBC micro:bit* (Apress), *Beginning LoRa Radio Networks with Arduino* (Apress), and *Building Arduino PLCs* (Apress).

Foreword

I worked for the BBC for 17 years, all of them in the BBC's Learning department, that part of the BBC responsible for developing materials for formal learning – students, teachers, and schools – and for all those people who just wanted to learn something new, what's called informal learning. In the last part of my BBC career, I ran BBC Learning's Innovation team, which is where I created the BBC micro:bit in response to the BBC's ambition to inspire its audience to engage with coding, computer technology, and digital creativity.

While leading the Innovation team, I was deeply interested in three literacies: digital literacy, media literacy and data literacy. I believe these literacies are vitally important to us, because, in the end, they are about citizenship, about providing a society's citizens with the tools to understand, safely live in and meaningfully contribute to their society and its cultures and to help shape the futures of those societies and cultures. In the world we live in, with its central focus on computer and digital technologies and its deep reliance on data, it seems to me digital and data literacies are core requirements for any citizen; they are disenfranchised without them, and any resource helping them effectively acquire them is much needed.

The BBC and its partners developed the BBC micro:bit to help children get to grips with digital literacy: to offer young people a simple, fun, and engaging way to develop digital skills and creativity that was physical in nature – something they could hold in their hands – and was low-cost enough to be given away. The BBC micro:bit was designed, from the outset, to be a learning tool, a device that would help young people start coding, making, and building, to help them think about something they wanted to produce and have the skills and tools to realize their ambitions. At its core, its aim was to support the development of a new generation of tech pioneers, to help today's young learners be the creators in our society, not just its mere consumers.

I never got the opportunity at the BBC to start thinking about tackling data literacy; however, I did have the satisfaction of believing the BBC micro:bit would probably be a useful learning tool with that too. The device was built to be used in a number of different curricula, the obvious ones like Computer Science, Science, Mathematics, and Design and Technology and the less obvious like Art, Music, and Dance. Our thinking was that in Computer Science it would help students understand how a computer worked and how to program one. However, in the other curricula, its use was intended to be different. In Science and Mathematics, we thought the micro:bit would enable the collection and analysis of scientific data. For Design and Technology, the micro:bit was a tool for invention – a device that would collect environmental or control data and make use of it in directing elements of a product. For Art, Music, and Dance, the micro:bit was to be a performance tool, a device for collecting various performance data, like the movement of an arm, and converting it to an artistic output, a musical sound, the color or intensity of a light, the movement of a brush – whatever the artist/performer wanted. The key micro:bit used in all these "other" curricula was always the same – the collection, analysis, and use of data.

When the partnership developed the BBC micro:bit, there was a huge temptation to build a device that could do everything, so every possible chip and sensor was on it. In the end, we realized that not only was this a cost issue – the micro:bit had to be as cheap as possible – but it was a learning and community issue. The micro:bit had to have space on it – it had to have inbuilt inability – so other people could develop it, add things to what it could do, make it better for themselves, and make it useful for the things they wanted to do.

All of this is why it is so satisfying to see this excellent book. The authors put the micro:bit to use exactly as we hoped, as one of a number of enablers, hopefully a very easy one, to help learners understand what it is to be a data scientist, while at the same time they recognized the BBC micro:bit is not perfect for its job. It has to be added to, built upon – and for this they use the clever XinaBox – while making sure there are always alternatives, including how things are coded. In doing all this, they also recognize, as the BBC micro:bit did, the person using their book is a learner, a novice. Things at the beginning have to be easy; they cannot be immediately overburdened with things not necessary to the core task, so they make sure knowledge of things, like circuit building and computer programming, are not barriers to using their book. At a personal level, I also really like the ethos behind the book. The authors believe the core driver for answering the questions posed in life is human curiosity, an inquisitive human mind, and, though they don't actually use the words, data literacy is a key skill for the world we live in.

As the book says, "We are all data scientists. On a daily basis, often without realizing it, we consume data. We use the information dished up to us constantly to make decisions, plans, or even just conversation... Understanding how to read and exploit data is a key skill in today's data driven society."

Howard Baker, 9 October 2019

CHAPTER 1

Introducing Data Science

A new day dawns. The alarm clock goes off and you leap out of bed, ready to face the world. You scan the weather report, settle on some clothes, grab a bite of breakfast – maybe cereal with milk. You might check a traffic update and then plan your route to school or work accordingly.

By the time your day has started you have already interacted with loads of different types of data – the time, the weather report, traffic updates, sports results and even the "right" amount of milk for the volume of cereal you poured. All driven by data. Data is such a normal part of our daily interaction with the world that we often do not give it a second thought. We are voracious consumers of data!

Where does all this data come from? If we are the consumers, who are the producers, and how do they do it? Where are the data factories? Why should we believe some data and not others, and how can we get smarter in how we use the data we are inundated with? Understanding how to read and take advantage of data is a key skill in today's data-driven society.

© Philip Meitiner, Pradeeka Seneviratne 2020
P. Meitiner and P. Seneviratne, *Beginning Data Science, IoT, and AI on Single Board Computers*,
https://doi.org/10.1007/978-1-4842-5766-1_1

1.1 Introducing Data Science

The longest journey begins with a single step. By the end of this book you will have a broad and solid grounding in the concepts that underlie theoretical and applied data science, but the first step is to ensure that this destination is clearly defined. What is "data science"?

The exact definition of data science is debated. We'll use the broadest possible definition and say that

Data science encompasses the activities associated with collecting, analyzing, interpreting, and acting on data.

If you count the number of eggs left in your fridge and work out which day of the week you will need to buy more, then you have performed an act of data science. Or if you estimate how many chocolate puddings are left in the canteen and how many people are ahead of you in the queue, then infer the likelihood of there being any left when you get to the front... again, data science! Even the activity of a teacher calling register in the morning form class, then again in the afternoon, and comparing the results has all the hallmarks of basic data science.

It is worth noting here that many people define data science more tightly and focus it on the analysis of data; most people who are identified as "data scientists" work primarily in the field of data analysis. For example, the textbook for data science at the University of Berkeley[1] tells us that data science "is about drawing useful conclusions from large and diverse data sets through exploration, prediction, and inference." It does not refer to the process of gathering those data sets or look in detail about how to use the data for anything besides making predictions. The definition we have adopted earlier does not contradict Berkeley or any commentator who would argue that data science is focused on data analysis. In this book

---

[1]This resource is available online and is a great follow-up to this book for people who want to read further. It can be found here: `www.inferentialthinking.com/chapters/intro`

we take a holistic overview and look at the activities that lead up to the analysis of data. You will see how the process of gathering data impacts on its analysis: how the experimental design introduces biases and factors that need to be understood and catered for. This book will show you that every element of the process is linked and that understanding the process will enrich your analysis.

In simple terms, data science is the process of converting **data** into **information**. The words **data** and **information** have formal meanings that are quite distinct. We'll illustrate these in **Table 1-1**.

Table 1-1. *Highlighting the differences between data and information*

	Data	Information
1	**Data** is the ingredients of a cake, the eggs, sugar, milk, etc.	**Information** is a slice of the cake.
2	If you ask 100 people whether they believe in climate change, you will have 100 units of **data**.	The statement "99% of people believe climate change needs to be addressed" is **information**.
3	**Data** is gathered or collected.	**Information** comes from analyzing data.
4	A **data** reading describes the state of something.	**Information** is a "fact" about something.

1.2 Using Temperature

One of the most common data measures, and one that we come into contact with daily, is temperature.

We usually have an idea of what the temperature is today, even if we haven't checked a weather report. We use temperature measures to cook our food and to maintain the air in our homes and workplaces at a comfortable level. When people are poorly we take their body temperature and when the temperature in an engine gets too hot we know there is something wrong.

We use temperature in this chapter because the reader will have an intuitive understanding of it: we don't need to try and explain what temperature is. But the concepts that we'll discuss, in this chapter and throughout the book, can be applied to any set of data: perhaps your data of choice is social media likes or stock market indicators, maybe sports results and leagues, or virus counts in blood cells, or the chilli heat of curry from your favorite curry shop. The principles of data science apply equally to all manner of data.

1.3 Measuring Temperature

Most humans (but not all) can sense temperature: we can feel the sun beating down on us in summer and our senses tell us the dangers of extreme hot and cold. We have a very rich subjective experience of the temperature and quite often strong opinions about it.

The first tool that measured temperature objectively was invented by Daniel Gabriel Fahrenheit in 1714. His mercury-based thermometer works from a very simple principle, which is shown in **Figure 1-1**.

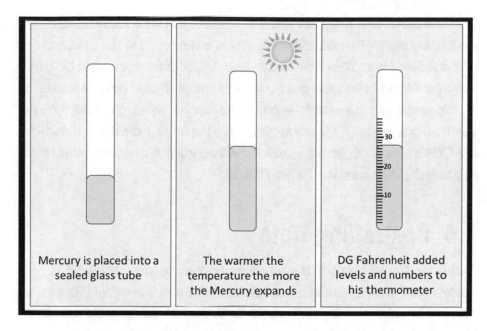

Mercury is placed into a
sealed glass tube

The warmer the
temperature the more
the Mercury expands

DG Fahrenheit added
levels and numbers to
his thermometer

Figure 1-1. Mercury in a closed glass container reacts to temperature

Warning   There are other ways to make thermometers – you can
even build one yourself with water and food coloring. Mercury is
especially effective but it is also a harmful element that has a toxic
effect, both on humans and on the environment. Thermometers that
use mercury are banned in places like hospitals and schools in many
countries around the world. The danger to humans comes from
breathing in mercury vapors, so if a mercury thermometer breaks
you will need to take great care in how you deal with it. Alcohol is the
most common alternative to mercury, but the principle of how the
thermometer works is the same whatever substance we put inside it.

When DG Fahrenheit invented the thermometer he also introduced a standard scale – Fahrenheit – which was widely used at the time and still is today. Alternative scales have been introduced since, with Celsius/ Centigrade and Kelvin the most common and preferred by data scientists.

To undertake the exercises in this chapter you need to acquire one or more thermometers – ideally analog ones, but any kind will do. We will use the Celsius scale, where 0 degrees is the freezing point of water and 100 degrees the temperature at which it boils.

1.4 Controlling Data

In this section we begin to design an experiment to investigate the temperature at different locations around your home or school (or similar place of interest). On the surface, this is an easy sounding assignment, but we will take some time to look at ways in which we can ensure our experimental design is of a high quality.

To gather data involves walking around taking temperature readings at various locations. In simple terms the process will go like this:

1.   Equip yourself with a list of locations and a thermometer.

2.   Walk to a specified location.

3.   Look at the thermometer.

4.   Write down the temperature.

5.   Go back to 2 and repeat until all locations have been measured.

This plan is simple but it has flaws. **Exercise 1-1** (outlined in **Table 1-2**) will show that when we measure temperature at a single location there are other factors which can influence the readings. We will undertake a quick activity that will help identify these **extraneous variables**.

Extraneous variables are factors that influence the data we collect but which are not related to the thing we are interested in. The ideal is to eliminate these from our experiment.

Table 1-2. *Guidelines for the temperature experiment activity*

Exercise 1-1	Controlling extraneous variables
Summary	Demonstrates the way in which extraneous variables can impact our readings, as well as ways to control these variables. It also trains us for Exercise 1-2.
Duration	5–10 minutes
Step-by-step process	1. Measure the temperature at different locations 2 in a single room. 2. Are there discrepancies in these values, and if so why? 3. Repeat: measure again but follow the guidelines outlined in the Additional Instructions section. 4. If you experienced discrepacies with the first round of measuring, were there similar discrepancies now? 5. Consider the differences in the approaches – was it worth the extra effort of the second method?
Additional Instructions	When reading the thermometer the second time (in step 3), follow this process: • Find a flat, wooden surface that is out of direct sunlight and not right next to it. The location should be away from breezes and not in any corners. • Place the thermometer down on the flat surface with the scale clearly visible. • Step back and wait for 30 seconds. • After 30 seconds read the temperature without touching or breathing on the thermometer.

(continued)

Table 1-2. (*continued*)

Exercise 1-1   Controlling extraneous variables

What we will learn	The effect of extraneous variables. How a "sloppy" data gathering process can result in unreliable data. The value in identifying and controlling extraneous variables and how a margin of error manifests. How a human being can have an impact on science.

The likelihood is that the preceding activity will have shown discrepancies – different temperature readings. How is this possible in a closed room – surely the temperature in the room is stable, so why aren't the readings all the same? There are a number of factors that might cause these discrepancies, such as:

- Putting a thermometer in direct sunlight will result in a higher reading than putting it in a shady spot.

- Holding a thermometer in your hand will impart some heat to it, which will change the reading.

- Some rooms will be naturally warmer/colder in different areas due to air flow and density of heat sources (e.g., people).

- Air sources – things such as a strong breeze, a fan, or an air conditioner – will affect the reading.

- Different thermometers might be calibrated differently, or they may be hard to read.

By detailing the process of reading the thermometer, as we did in the Additional Instructions section of the activity, we have reduced the impact of these extraneous variables by keeping them consistent across all measurements. In data science terminology, we have **controlled** those variables. Some data scientists might say that we have eliminated some of the "noise" from the data.

1.5 Understanding the Tools

Throughout this book we are going to use increasingly more complex tools to measure a variety of different data types. Even with a simple mercury thermometer it is important to understand exactly what your tools are measuring.

A thermometer reads **ambient** temperature – the temperature in the immediate vicinity of the thermometer. For this experiment we want to measure the temperature in a location (such as a room), but what we are actually measuring is the temperature in a limited area around the thermometer.

Understanding how a measuring tool works allows us to identify factors that might influence our readings – that might impact on the quality of our data. Our thermometer measures ambient temperature, not the temperature of a room; we need to look out for factors that might make this ambient temperature different from the room temperature. We need to ensure that the small area of space we actually measure is typical of the wider space that we are interested in. We can use this knowledge to design data collection strategies that provide higher-quality data.

1.6 Data Quality

We collect data so that it can be used, and it is self-evident that high-quality data will be more useful than low-quality data, all other things being equal. GIGO: garbage in, garbage out. But what makes one set of data "higher quality" than another set?

To judge the quality of data, we look at its **validity** and **reliability**.

The **validity** of data refers to the extent to which it measures what we want it to measure. We are trying to measure the temperature of a location, but we are actually measuring the temperature around the thermometer. Is it valid to say that the temperature readings we have taken apply to the location in which they were taken?

Reliable data can be replicated. So, if several people all measure the temperature in the same location at the same time, we would expect them to all get the same result. Where this happens, we say that the data is reliable.

When we know that two data points are both **reliable** and **valid**, we can compare them to other similarly reliable and valid data and have some confidence in any observations we make. So if I measure the temperature at my desk in the United Kingdom and it is 25 degrees, and if an astronaut measures the temperature on the International Space Station (ISS) and finds that it is 23 degrees, then I can be pretty sure that it is warmer at my desk than on the ISS.

If we don't control the extraneous variables then our data is not so valid and reliable. Does that mean it is useless? In real-world experiments not all extraneous variables can be controlled. To perform real-world experimentation data scientists have come up with clever techniques to extract valuable insights, even from low-quality data. The trick lies in identifying and understanding the extraneous variables that are influencing our data and then making allowances for their influence when we analyze the data. Consider the following example:

Temperature records dating all the way back to the 19th century have been compared to help show incontrovertible evidence of climate change. Over the years the measuring equipment has been replaced, maybe even changed or upgraded, and the locations where measures are taken have either changed completely or the surroundings are now very different. All these factors are likely to have some impact on the measurements – they are extraneous variables and it is impossible to control these fully. To address situations like this data scientists use what is called a **margin of error**, which is an estimation of just how **reliable** their data is. So, if there is a margin of error of 2 in a thermometer reading of 20 degrees, a data scientist will understand that the actual temperature is most likely somewhere between 18 degrees and 22 degrees.

We've looked at how to use our thermometers to gather quality data, but before we undertake our first experiment let's have a quick look at capturing (or recording) that data.

1.7 Data Capturing

The experiment that we are planning will require us to record a number of different temperature values. Human memory being what it is it makes sense to write down the readings when we take them.

This process – writing down or recording our data readings – is referred to as **capturing** or **gathering** data. There are a load of different ways you can record data, but the standard approach is to use a **data table**.

Chances are you familiar with the idea of information being presented in the form of a table: we've already used a couple tables in this book. **Table 1-3** outlines the key features of a data table.

Table 1-3. *Key features of a data table*

Feature	Description	True or false
1	A table is a made up of columns and rows.	True
2	Where the rows and columns cross, each rectangle is called a cell. This paragraph is in a cell.	True
3	For data science we usually write data, in the form of numbers, in each cell. But we also put text into tables, like we are doing here.	True
4	Usually tables have a few columns and each column is used for different types of data, like this table.	True
5	Tables usually have more rows than columns.	True
6	As you collect more and more data, you add more and more rows to the table. You only add columns when you start to collect new types of data.	True
7	When you have some data that is linked, such as location name and the temperature at that location, you add it to the same row.	True
8	If you know how to use a table, you know all you need to know about tables to work through this book.	True

Ask yourself two questions about the preceding table:

1. **Were you able to follow the way the information was presented?** If so your knowledge of tables is adequate to continue with the chapter.

2. **Did you wonder what the point of the first and third columns was?** If so, good spotting – they were useless – your knowledge of tables is adequate to continue with the chapter.

Tables are one of those things that are hard to explain but which most people are able to use. For now, we just need to capture data into tables. In the exercise in the following section we will use a data table that has three columns:

1. **Location** – Write down the names of the locations in this column.

2. **Temperature** – Write down the temperature in this one.

3. **Notes** – Use the Notes column to write down observations that might be relevant to the experiment.

Draw up a table to capture the data. Allow for 12 rows or so and try to pick a nice variety of locations – we want some variation in our data. **Table 1-4** shows what it will look like.

Table 1-4. *A blank data capturing form for Exercise 1-2*

Location	Temperature	Notes

Use the table by writing a location in the left-hand column and then writing the temperature at that location in the middle column. The Notes column is used to jot down observations that might be of interest to our experiment and can be left blank for some locations. Table 1-5 shows what a completed table might look like.

Table 1-5. *An illustration of a filled-in table from Exercise 1-2*

Location	Temperature	Notes
Staffroom	22.5	Perfectly air conditioned with large comfy couches
The canteen	24	Unable to find a flat wooden surface for the thermometer
The library	20.5	Has air conditioning
Big tree in playground	16	Was an overcast day
Ms. Smith's classroom	22.5	Classroom faces the sunny side of the school
Ms. Cohen's classroom	22	
Mr. Nkomo's classroom	21	There were three fans blowing in the classroom

1.8 Experimenting with Temperature

In this section we undertake the activity of capturing temperature data in a number of locations and then, in the following section, we will analyze the data we capture. We will refer to the whole process as an **experiment**.

This section outlines our **experimental design**, which is the set of instructions and guidelines we will follow to perform the experiment. We saw earlier that the validity and reliability of our data are important – having a clear and well-planned experimental design helps us to control some extraneous variables and gives us more reliable and valid data.

We recommend you take temperature readings from a number of different locations, inside and outside. The ideal outcome is to have around a dozen readings and to ensure that there is a fair range in results.

If you don't have access to a range of locations, an alternative would be to take temperature readings from the same location at different times, or use a medical thermometer to measure the temperature of soil around different plants. You could even undertake this exercise with a different type of data – substitute temperature for UV light levels, CO_2 or anything that you can measure and which you find interesting (**Table 1-6**).

Table 1-6. *Outline for Exercise 1-2*

Exercise 1-2	Comparing the temperature of different locations
Summary	The temperature at a number of different locations will be measured and recorded; then the data will be analyzed. We will analyze both the results and the quality of the experimental design of this activity.
Duration	30 mins
Preparation	• Round up some thermometers – they don't need to be perfect – discrepancies and data issues are OK. • Prepare a list of locations. Choose ones that are likely to have some variances in temperature – inside and outside if possible. • Draw a data table to use to capture the data. Write in the location names and add any notes that might be of value (e.g., identify extraneous variables).
Step-by-step process	1. Visit each location specified. 2. Read the thermometer using the guidelines specified in the following Additional Instructions. 3. The temperature is recorded in each location. 4. Go back to 1 and repeat until all locations have been measured. 5. Once all the data has been gathered, move on to Section 1.9 and work through the questions and topics listed there.

(*continued*)

Table 1-6. (*continued*)

Exercise 1-2	Comparing the temperature of different locations
Additional Instructions	When reading the thermometer, follow this process: • Find a flat, wooden surface that is out of direct sunlight and not right next to it. The location should be away from breezes and not in any corners. • Place the thermometer down on the flat surface with the scale clearly visible. • Step back and wait for 30 seconds. • After 30 seconds, read the temperature without touching or breathing on the thermometer.
What we will learn	The data gathering process will be fun, but a bit tedious: human time is precious. This is a key driver toward digital tools, which we introduce in the next chapter. Participants will undertake an analysis of the data by working through the questions and topics listed in the next section – they will see how asking questions of the data can provide interesting and unique information.

1.9 Analyzing Our Results

We have a table of data collected with some care according to a plan we put together to ensure our data is as reliable and valid as possible. It probably isn't perfect, but it is fair to say that most people would have a little more confidence in this data than they would if we had not put a plan in place.

This table is a **raw** data set – freshly gathered and ready to be used in our analysis. Rather than try and define what analysis is, let's just do some!

We are going to look at our data set and see what information we can extract from it. What we will try to do is describe the data in English sentences that have some meaning: we are going to turn the table of data into snippets of conversation. For example:

- "The hottest place in the school is..."

- "If you want to cool down go and sit ..."

- "The data collection method was flawed in this way... "

Data analysis is part science, part art:

- The science part includes tools and techniques that have been developed over many years, some of which we will look at later on in this book.

- The art part is the inquisitive human mind thinking of interesting questions and looking at whether a data set contains insights that will help answer those questions.

It is probably safe to say that the single most important element of data analysis is human curiosity.

With the data set that we have just collected you should now ask, and try to answer, the questions listed below. Formulate the answers as statements, in plain English, that you might drop into a conversation, or in an email, or perhaps as a social media update. Listen out for anything that sounds interesting.

We can't really provide answers to these questions for you: imagine working through this book in Sri Lanka in high summer, or Iceland in the winter months, or in your local neighborhood. The answers are going to be different everywhere – you will be working on a totally unique data set and your conclusions will be original.

The questions are grouped into categories.

Analysis of Extremities

With pretty much any set of data we can usually learn something by looking at the extreme values. Ask these sorts of questions:

- Where was the hottest location?

- Where was the coldest?

- If they are different, why? What makes one location warmer or colder than the other?

- What is the range of temperatures? How different is the hottest and the coldest locations? What can we infer from this?

Analysis of Averages (Central Tendency)

We will look at averages in more detail in Chapter 5. For now, ask:

- What is the average temperature of the school/area you analyzed?

- How useful is the average? How many locations were there where the temperature was equal to the average? What does it really tell us?

- If we decide the average is useful, is it midway between the extremes or is it closer to one or the other? Either way, does this tell us anything?

Random Insights

Also look for insights in the data by asking questions such as:

- Could you identify ways to cut down on heating/cooling? Are fans/heaters/air conditioners in the best locations.

- Are there any problem locations that need attention? Is there a particular area that is not comfortable?

- If there are several locations that are not comfortable, is there a single reason?

- Does the temperature affect behavior? How would you investigate this?

- Where would you go to eat an ice cream, and where would you go to eat soup?

Analysis of Data Quality

We should always question the quality of our data:

- What factors in our experiment might impact on the reliability of the data? And which might impact on its validity? How does this change our answers?

- Are the answers we have decided on in our analysis logical – do they make sense? Do we believe them?

- **Double check anything unusual!** A lot of researchers will tell you that data that looks unusual is often interesting, but the first response to interesting data is to check for errors.

- If your experiment included two or more groups, check how similar is the data across different groups? How can any differences be explained?

- Do we think there is a margin of error in our results? If so, how much?

Introspection

And with any experiment, ask how you can improve it:

- How can you make it more efficient (i.e., save human time/effort)? Consider technological solutions throughout.

- Can we make our experiment more environmentally friendly?

- How could we make our data more valid and reliable?

- Is there is a trade-off between efficiency and making our data more reliable/valid? If so, what should we do differently next time?

- Could we scale it up? How many locations could we sample in 1 hour? If there are upper limits, how do we overcome these?

- How could we build on the experiment? For example, how would you design the experiment so that it takes a different reading every half an hour throughout the day?

- Were there any ethical implications?

Did you find that any of the answers to the preceding questions were interesting or useful? It only takes one or two insights to make it all worthwhile.

We will look at data analysis in more detail in later chapters — for now, bear in mind that at the root of all data analysis is a set of questions such as the ones asked earlier.

1.10 Summary

We are all data scientists. On a daily basis, often without realizing it, we consume data. We use the information dished up to us constantly to make decisions, plans or even just conversation.

In this chapter we had a quick overview of the whole journey that data goes on: from an experimental design to being collected using some tools, to being analyzed and converted into information.

To delve further into data science we are going to need access to more sophisticated tools than mercury thermometers. In Chapter 2 we will look at ways that we can build our own instruments to measure data.

CHAPTER 2

Data Science Goes Digital

In this chapter we will identify a set of electronic components with which we will build a range of different digital tools. These tools will be used to gather data, which is essential fuel for our journey into data science.

2.1 Making It Digital

Did you know that every single teenager on the planet was born in the twenty-first century, after the creation of the Internet, email, even Google? Many of the children growing up today have never known the absence of digital magic. We are living in a digital world – it crept up on some of us, but more and more of us are being born into it. People even refer to our current epoch as the Digital or Information Age, acknowledgment of the extent to which information is woven into every aspect of our lives. The digital revolution – the replacement of analog technology with digital equivalents – laid the foundation for our modern society.

Although the analog thermometer served us well in **Chapter 1**, to learn more about data science we are going to need access to increasingly complex data sets: we will collect hundreds, thousands, or even millions of data points as our experiments get more ambitious. Our analog thermometer is not fit for this purpose, and the same is true of other analog tools. We are going to need access to sophisticated digital tools to make this journey possible.

© Philip Meitiner, Pradeeka Seneviratne 2020
P. Meitiner and P. Seneviratne, *Beginning Data Science, IoT, and AI on Single Board Computers*,
https://doi.org/10.1007/978-1-4842-5766-1_2

2.2 Measuring Temperature Digitally

In **Chapter 1** we saw how an analog thermometer works; the fundamental principle is the same for a digital one. Ambient temperature causes something to react, to change, and this change is observed in some way:

- In an analog thermometer, the visible level of mercury changes.

- In a digital tool the reaction is converted into an electrical signal that a computer (or microprocessor) can perceive and interpret.

Figure 2-1 shows the different components that constitute a digital thermometer. It is a very basic **"circuit"** or **"block diagram"** in a style that is used throughout this book.

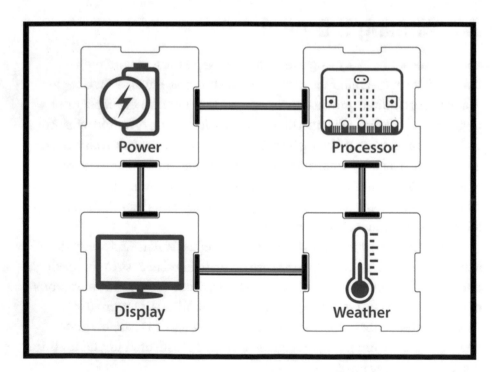

Figure 2-1. *Core components of a digital thermometer*

Any digital thermometer will have the following components:

1. **A power source**: Digital circuits require electrical power.

2. **A microprocessor**: The role it plays is explained in more detail below.

3. **A temperature sensor**: When power/electricity is supplied to a temperature sensor it will react to the ambient temperature around it. The sensor transmits data about its state through the circuit and it plays the same role as the mercury in an analog thermometer.

4. **A way of outputting the temperature data**: For example, on a screen.

5. **These need to be connected together somehow**: The lines joining the components are also important.

The Role of the Microprocessor

A microprocessor can be compared to the brain of a baby: full of potential but unable to actually do anything. A baby learns how to perform basic actions through being taught, and we **"teach"** our microprocessor how to perform basic actions by loading a computer program onto it.

The microprocessor is the **"brain"** of the circuit. Electricity flows through the circuit, and it is the microprocessor which **"monitors"** this electricity, interprets any data encoded into it, and then acts on it. To perform as a thermometer:

- The microprocessor knows it needs to **"listen"** for any signals coming from the temperature sensor: it knows this because someone, perhaps us, has **"programmed"** it to do just that. When a signal is received from the sensor, the microprocessor is able to convert that signal into a usable data point: a temperature reading.

- The microprocessor also knows how to send information to the screen to make it show words and numbers: it knows this because, again, it has been told how in the program. It will send a signal to the screen that will make it display the temperature. Someone, perhaps us, has programmed/told the microprocessor what information to show on the screen and how to display it.

2.3 Building Digital Tools

Do we really need to know how to build digital tools to become data scientists? In the professional world a data scientist doesn't need to be a toolmaker:

- There are many off-the-shelf products that will meet your data gathering needs. You can buy weather monitors, CO2 monitors and apps that tell you the temperature.

- A team that is undertaking data science might have specialists in many fields, all responsible for different parts of the process: someone else might build data gathering tools.

- You could commission someone to gather the data for you. Lots of businesses will sell you all manner of data. Or use online tools.

This book is written for people who do not have access to those methods; we will have to collect data ourselves and we will build the data gathering tools that we need.

Knowing how to build a digital tool is always going to be a useful skill, but it is clearly not a core skill of data science. The field of data science encompasses many disciplines: the data analyst, the toolmaker, the data collector, the project manager, and the experiment designer, to name a few. All their contributions play a role in the data science process. In this book we learn just enough about circuit building to enable us to build the tools we need to explore data science. We'll show you how to do this without needing to become engineers first: it is not necessary to have any prior knowledge of circuit building (or computer programming) to work through this book.

2.4 Using the BBC micro:bit As a Thermometer

Did you know that the BBC micro:bit has a built-in temperature sensor? It is easy to use and means that the micro:bit can be programmed to behave like a thermometer, which is what we are about to do.

We've seen how understanding a measuring tool helps us to understand the data that it yields:

When the BBC micro:bit was built they did not include a temperature sensor on the board. It was only after it had been designed that one of the engineers realized there was a chip on the micro:bit with a built-in heat sensor, and that it was possible to access the temperature from that. There is a similar story about how someone realized that the light sensitivity of the LED matrix could be used as a crude sensor.

To use the micro:bit as a thermometer we will have to write some code, which we will then **copy** (or **flash**) onto the micro:bit. Every digital tool that we build will need to be coded.

2.5 Coding Guidelines Used in This Book

Throughout the book we are going to build ever more sophisticated digital tools to help us develop our data science skills, and each tool will need to have code written for it. When it comes to coding the tools we will always provide two options:

1. **The no-code option**: Go to our **resource website** (http://xib.one/XB) and find **"Section X.Y".** You will see a hex file that you can download and flash straight onto your micro:bit. Instructions are on the page. Throughout the book, we will offer you **"no-code"** solutions.

2. **An option that you can code yourself:** Where possible we will use **Microsoft MakeCode**, which is a fun and easy-to-use **block code editor**. Where MakeCode does not provide the functionality we need **MicroPython** is used. We will use the **Mu editor** for our MicroPython coding.

If you choose to write your own code we will show you first the **natural language code**: a step-by-step description of the process required to achieve our goals, written in natural language. We will then show you the **MakeCode** blocks (or **MicroPython** code) needed to turn that **natural language code** into real code that will work on your micro:bit. This approach makes it easier to adapt the code to different hardware platforms or different coding languages: the natural language code serves as a simple but adequate software specification.

2.6 Using the micro:bit Code Editors

If you choose to write the code yourself then you need to choose a code editor. There are several options for the BBC micro:bit; we will provide guidelines for MakeCode and Mu (MicroPython).

The purpose of this book is not to introduce you to coding on the BBC micro:bit – there are many great books you can use for that. But for those of you who are new to coding on the BBC micro:bit there are a few key topics that you will need to understand. You will be able to read up on them in links from our **resource website** (`http://xib.one/XB`).

2.7 Using the "No-Code" Option

Not everyone who needs to use a weather station wants to write the code for it themselves. In some situations coding is an important skill, while in others it is irrelevant: building a weather station in a computer science class and in a geography class will be approached in completely different ways and will have very different learning outcomes. And of course, the focus of this book is on data science: the tools we build and the code we write for them are just enablers – we need them to tell the data science story properly, but they are not the heroes of the story.

The no-code option, along with the easy-to-build system of components that we describe later in this chapter, will allow you to get your digital tools up and running in minutes. You will just need to build the tool as described, and then download the code from the URL provided.

And don't think of this as cheating! You don't program a new fridge when you buy one, nor are you expected to code your car before you drive it. So why should you have to program a data gathering tool?

2.8 Coding the micro:bit Thermometer

We will now build our micro:bit thermometer.

The circuit for this is very simple – just a micro:bit and a power supply (**Figure 2-2**). We don't need anything extra as we are going to use the micro:bit's onboard temperature sensor and the 5x5 LED matrix to display the temperature.

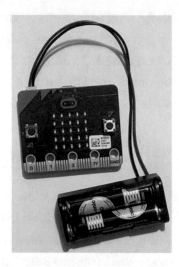

Figure 2-2. *micro:bit thermometer – just a micro:bit and a power supply (2xAAA battery pack)*

There are several ways to power your micro:bit, the most common being:

1. You can plug your micro:bit into a USB socket using a cable.

2. You can plug the 2xAAA battery pack that is supplied with the micro:bit into the available connection port.

There is more detail on this in our **resource website** (http://xib.one/XB). A number of the digital tools we will build need to be portable, so you should ensure you have the micro:bit battery pack and some batteries available.

We will need to write code to tell the micro:bit how to act as a thermometer: **Figure 2-3** presents the **"natural language code"** for this.

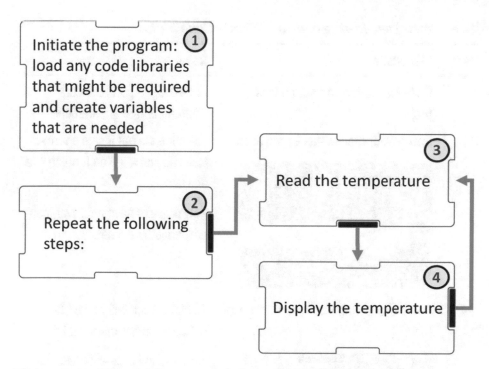

Figure 2-3. *Natural language code for a digital thermometer*

No-code option: You can find a precompiled version of the code needed for this section on our **resource website**. Go to http://xib.one/XB and search for **Section 2.8**.

Table 2-1 shows how to convert the **natural language code** from earlier into MakeCode blocks that can be compiled and loaded onto your micro:bit.

Table 2-1. *Developing code with MakeCode blocks*

Step	MakeCode	Notes
1	Open MakeCode and start a new project.	MakeCode imports the core micro:bit library automatically.
2	Ensure your project has a forever loop: forever	The code we put inside a forever loop will just keep on running over and over. New projects have a forever loop preloaded by default.
3 & 4	Add the following blocks to the forever loop: show string "Temp C: " show number temperature (°C)	The first block will make "Temp C:" scroll on the micro:bit LEDs. The second block will make the temperature scroll on the micro:bit LEDs.

Figure 2-4 shows the full MakeCode program for the micro:bit thermometer.

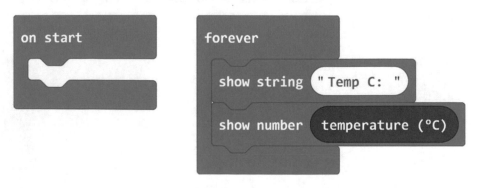

Figure 2-4. *MakeCode blocks for the micro:bit thermometer*

Now that the code has been written you just need to compile it and download ("flash") it onto your micro:bit. Check our **resource website** (http://xib.one/XB) if you are unsure of how to do so.

Once the flashing process has been completed, the temperature in Celsius will display on the 5x5 LED matrix, scrolling continually. The output will look something like **Figure 2-5**.

Figure 2-5. *A temperature reading scrolling on a micro:bit from right to left. Each micro:bit image represents a single frame of the output*

The code we have put onto the micro:bit tells it how to behave as a digital thermometer. We have built our first digital tool; now it's time to use it.

2.9 Comparing Analog and Digital Thermometers

We are going to undertake a quick exercise, described in **Table 2-2**, where we will read temperature simultaneously from a micro:bit and an analog thermometer and then compare our results.

Table 2-2. *Details for Exercise 2-1*

Exercise 2-1	What is the temperature in the room?
Summary	We measure the temperature in a room using different tools, ideally read by a number of different people. Values will be different: the micro:bit temperature sensor reads hotter than the air almost all the time so is likely to be higher than the analog readings.
	This exercise is designed to reveal insights about data quality and the tools being used while introducing the concept of aggregating data. How can we resolve all the different results into a single measure: what *is* the temperature in the room?
Duration	10–15 minutes
Step-by-step process	1. Acquire at least 1 micro:bit thermometer and an analog thermometer.
	2. Read the temperature from both devices in a variety of locations in a room and write them down in a table.
	3. As discrepancies are revealed, consider hypotheses about the source.
	4. When you have collected the data, work through the points listed in **Section 2.9**.
What we will learn	We apply what we've learned about data quality to analyze our results and try to make sense out of discrepancies.
	By trying to agree on what the temperature of the room is, we are introduced to aggregation and range.
	We also learn how to use the micro:bit tool we designed to gather data.

2.10 Analysis

In later chapters we are going to look at some of the tools you can use to enhance your analysis. But analysis always starts with curiosity – quite often with questions, such as these:

"Is the air quality in my neighborhood poor?"

"Is the lake getting lower every year?"

"How far is it to the moon?"

Work through the topics in the following sections.

Analysis of Extremities

Look at the maximum and minimum values for the micro:bit and the analog readings. The **range** is the difference between the maximum and the minimum. Which tool has the greatest range, and why might that be? What does this tell us, does it tell us anything? Is a smaller or larger range ideal? Why? This all links this back to the reliability/validity of the data.

Having a broad range could just reflect that different areas of the room are at different temperatures. In general, though, a smaller range can indicate higher accuracy – if the room is a stable temperature throughout, then accurate thermometers would have a tight range.

But something else comes into play with our micro:bits: their thermometers measure the operating heat of the chip on which they are mounted, and this is usually higher than room temperature. So they MAY show a tighter range, but perhaps because they are less sensitive to ambient temperature.

Analysis of Averages: "Central Tendency"

Is there actually a perfect, right answer to the question: *what is the temperature in this room*? If so, which parts of the room are that exact temperature? What is the single value we would choose to describe the temperature of this room? An average is a convenient and useful summary of a large set of numbers.

Analysis of Data Quality

Is one of our thermometers right? Or is one more right than the other? Remember to link this back to what the tool is actually measuring.

BOTH are right in relation to what they are measuring – if there is an error, it is because we have **extrapolated**. When we extrapolate, we take a value that means something and we apply it to something else.

So, when we take a temperature value that applies to a very small volume of the room and we apply that to the whole room, we have extrapolated the data. Extrapolating can impact on the validity of data: the more we extrapolate, the less valid we risk the data becoming.

Introspection

What could be improved if we were to repeat the exercise?

There aren't really any right and wrong answers to the questions earlier; the value of the exercise is in the questioning and the discussion – getting into the habit of asking loads of questions about a data set. This is the heart of the data analysis phase.

Data analysis does get a bit more formal. The professional tools of data analysis are very sophisticated and the mathematics that backs it up is complicated and elegant. But whatever tool you use, data analysis means asking questions and then finding answers. To a data scientist a set of data is like an unopened box of chocolates, a treat, ready to be cracked and discovered. But first, always check the ingredients!

2.11 Why the micro:bit?

In the previous section the analog thermometer was probably slightly easier to use and most likely a little more accurate; if all we ever wanted to do was measure the temperature then there is no compelling reason to switch to the micro:bit.

Moving forward we are going to stick with digital tools: digital means that we have access to a huge range of hardware, software and knowledge that we can use to great effect in our data science experiments.

Imagine building a tool that reads pollen levels and then uploads them in real time to a website that tracks the levels as you walk around. Add in a warning light if the level is too high, get a few dozen people using it at the same time and get your route updated live to take you through the areas least likely to set off an allergy you might have. That is applied data science, and it is the promise of being able to do that sort of really cool stuff that makes us stick with digital tools.

The BBC micro:bit might not make a great thermometer but it meets our needs for a microprocessor in many ways:

- It is a very easy microprocessor to use – it's more user friendly than any other option out there.

- The coding editors are very easy to use.

- A lot of people already have them (there are almost 5 million in circulation) and more are bring produced all the time. It is a growing platform, especially in education.

- It is well supported – lots of materials and help.

- It also has a bit of a cool factor: *from the makers of* **Doctor Who**, *here comes the BBC micro:bit*!

We are going to use the BBC micro:bit throughout this book, but when we list the hardware requirements we will suggest alternatives. You can follow this book just as easily with a Circuit Playground, Raspberry Pi or Arduino device at hand.

The BBC micro:bit by itself is not going to meet all of our needs though – our experience in this chapter has already shown us a couple of shortcomings:

- It includes a temperature sensor as well as a magnetometer and an accelerometer, but there are no other environmental sensors. We need access to a broader set of sensors that we can use to gather interesting data.

- The 5x5 LED matrix is not very good for reading lots of data. At some point, we are going to need other methods to get the data out of the micro:bit.

We are going to go digital and we are going to use the BBC micro:bit as the microprocessor in our digital toolkit. We are also going to need to enhance it with some other kit to gather all the data we'll need.

2.12 What Kit Do We Need?

Every digital measuring device has a number of common features: they are made up of the same basic components. Throughout this book when we describe how to build the devices we'll use a circuit/block diagram such as **Figure 2-1** (shown earlier) and **Figure 2-6** to show you the hardware components that are included. Using these circuit/block diagrams you can build your tools/instruments using whatever hardware you have access to. **Figure 2-6** shows an example of a circuit built with seven components.

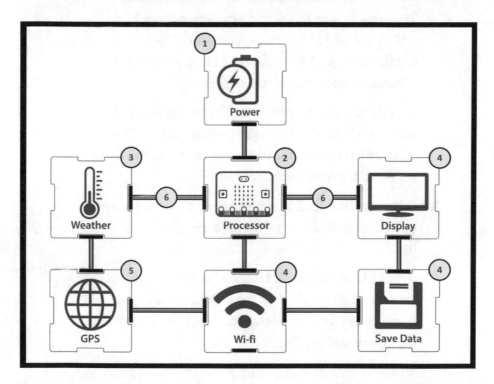

Figure 2-6. *A simple rendition of the components of a sophisticated digital tool*

The tools we build in this book will include most of the following components:

1. **A power source**: We will use the 2xAAA battery holder or the USB cable that comes with the micro:bit for power.

2. **A microprocessor**: We are going to use the BBC micro:bit.

3. **One or more sensors**: Sensors to measure things. There are a huge range of digital sensors available, and by the end of this book, you should feel confident enough to source a specific sensor and use it to create a digital measuring tool.

4. **Several ways to output data**: The image shows us using an OLED display, a file system, and Wi-Fi – three different ways we can access the data that is collected from the sensors.

5. Other **cool stuff**: Like GPS or actuators (which move or control things: e.g. start a motor or turn on a light).

6. **A way of connecting it all up**: When all the pieces are connected, we have a **"circuit."** The way that components are joined together is a key element of the circuit and is often not trivial.

The instrument shown in **Figure 2-5** would make a great weather monitoring tool. The GPS module would allow us to **geo-tag** our results to identify the location where readings are taken. The Wi-Fi module would be used to upload data from the instrument to an Internet of Things (IoT) platform as well as allowing us to get the real time, which would be used to **timestamp** the data (when a data reading is taken the time of the reading is also recorded). Data is saved locally on the memory card in case the Wi-Fi connection drops out. We need a toolkit that will allow us to build data gathering instruments of this complexity.

2.13 Selecting Our Toolkit

Most electronics retailers will stock the components we need: we are just a Google search away from being able to make some really cool and quite unique tools.

But unless you are familiar with the world of microcomputing the array of options will be daunting. From beginners to seasoned makers, the following questions always make purchases a bit stressful:

- How do we know which ones to buy? There are dozens of CO2 sensors on the market – which ones are appropriate for our needs?

- How can we be sure the bits we buy will work together? Will the components all be **compatible**? What is the right voltage, and what is voltage anyway? Do they all speak the same kind of binary, or are there dialects? Do I cut the red wire or the green one?

- A related challenge is **connectivity** – how do the components actually fit together? How are we supposed to join them?

To avoid these sorts of concerns, as well as avoiding the need to learn anything about circuits, we are going to use components from the **XinaBox** range to supplement our BBC micro:bit. This range is suitable for our needs in a number of ways:

- It is compatible with micro:bit and can be coded easily through MakeCode and MicroPython.

- Components can be joined with connectors – we can make circuits as easily as building with Lego. There is no need to learn anything about circuit building.

- It provides all the components we will need throughout this book.

- It is simple to **"map"** components to our needs. Want to add Wi-Fi? There is an xChip for that. LoRa, or GPS, or Bluetooth? There is an xChip for that. A sensor that measures UV light, or motion, or CO_2 levels? There is an xChip for that. And they all connect together the same way.

Using this system allows us to focus on the core skills of data science – we don't need to spend ages learning how to build complex circuits with soldering irons, breadboards, and cables. That is fun and is a great skill to have, but it is not what this book is about.

Figure 2-7 shows a micro:bit sitting in an **IM01 bridge**.

Figure 2-7. *The micro:bit slips easily into the XinaBox IM01 bridge*

Figures 2-8 and **2-9** show the two **xChips** connected together. IDs are clearly visible (OD01 on the left and SW01 on the right).

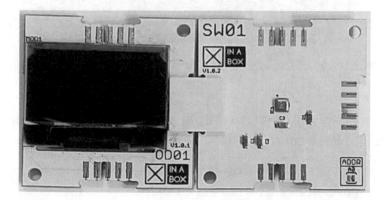

Figure 2-8. *Using the xBus connectors, xChips can be clipped together easily. Just make sure the ID is always facing up*

Figure 2-9. *Clip the xChips to the bridge and you have built a digital tool*

For those of you who do not use micro:bit or do not have access to XinaBox kit, please note that

- Although every activity is solved using micro:bit and the XinaBox kit, we present an alternative hardware solution each time and the natural language code should be easy to adapt.

- The hardware in the activities is described in a generic way – if you can build the circuits described, whatever system you use, then you should be able to follow the book.

2.14 Guide to Hardware Requirements

Throughout the book, we will undertake a series of increasingly more complex experiments. Each of these will require us to gather data, and we will need to build a tool to do so. We will define the components needed in this tool in a "Hardware Requirements" section which will include the following details:

1. A simple block/circuit diagram will be shown identifying the components used in our tool. **Figure 2-1** and **Figure 2-6** are examples of these.

2. A table will list these components – **Table 2-3** is an example. We list the components from the block/circuit diagram in the column **What we need**. We also list the hardware we use in the book in the **What we will use** column. The third column, **Alternative hardware**, shows a different hardware setup that you could use to build the same tool.

Table 2-3. *An example of the Hardware Requirements component list table*

What we need	What we will use	Alternative hardware
Power	micro:bit 2xAAA battery pack	USB cable
Microprocessor	micro:bit	Adafruit Circuit Playground
Weather sensor	XinaBox SW01 xChip	Any device with a mounted Bosch BME280 chip
Display	XinaBox OD01 OLED screen	micro:bit 5x5 LED matrix
Connectivity	XinaBox IM01 bridge and xBus connectors	Edge connector breakout, breadboard and hookup wires

Figure 2-10 shows a **"tool"** built with the hardware listed in the **What we will use** column in **Table 2-3**.

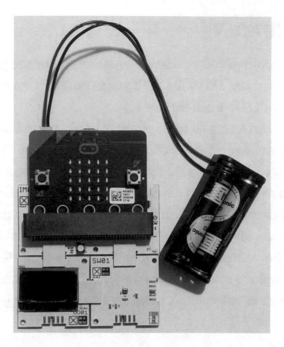

Figure 2-10. *A tool built with the hardware listed in the "What we will use" column*

All the code that is provided (no-code, MakeCode, and MicroPython) will work with the hardware described in the **What we will use** column in **Table 2-3**.

You may need to adapt the code slightly if you use different hardware. In particular, most manufacturers will provide libraries (or extensions) for you to use with their kit. If you use different hardware, look on the manufacturer's website for information on how to find and use the appropriate libraries. Adding them to your workspace should be similar to how it is described in our website.

2.15 Summary

To undertake meaningful data science experiments we are going to need to gather our own data. This will require us to build digital data gathering tools which we will also need to code.

We have chosen a very simple system of hardware to build our tools with and have provided a variety of options to code them. This includes the no-code option, which is intended to make the data gathering tools useful to people who are not keen on writing code themselves: being a computer programmer and engaging with digital technology are not the same thing.

The system we will use is the BBC micro:bit + XinaBox "xChips". It is hard to find a simpler option, short of buying ready-made tools that will perform the functions we need. With this system we can embark on our data science journey without any prior hardware knowledge.

CHAPTER 3

Experimenting with Weather

In this chapter we are going to design an experiment where we will record temperature, humidity and atmospheric pressure. We'll use our digital toolkit to build a weather station, and then we'll investigate how those measures impact on our day-to-day perception of the weather.

3.1 Introduction

If you had to pick the single most important concept within data science it would probably be **correlations**:

> *When two different data sets are correlated it means that they will usually behave in ways that are mutually predictable: by observing one data set we can make predictions about the other data set. We have an intuitive understanding of correlations: we know it gets cooler at night, so there is a correlation between the time of day and the temperature; we also take it for granted that taller people tend to weigh a bit more than shorter people, all other things being equal. A lot of what we call "common sense" is built on these sorts of real-world correlations. We will look at correlations in more detail in **Chapter** 5.*

P. Meitiner and P. Seneviratne, *Beginning Data Science, IoT, and AI on Single Board Computers*, https://doi.org/10.1007/978-1-4842-5766-1_3

Discovering correlations in data is exciting and can lead to very interesting, sometimes groundbreaking, insights. We are going to collect a load of data and then search it for correlations.

3.2 Measuring Weather

Humans have a sense of the weather – our experience of it is visceral – we can feel it. It can make or break our moods, save or doom whole civilizations and turn a dream day into a lifelong regret. And, of course, those beautiful rainbows!

Weather is a fundamental human experience; with climate change disrupting weather patterns all over the world and bringing extreme events the need to study it grows increasingly urgent. The more we understand the weather the better we can predict it and maybe even control it. But this understanding begins with data, which we are going to collect. So how do we measure **"the weather"**?

Climate/weather scientists use a variety of measures such as temperature, humidity, atmospheric pressure, light levels, soil moisture, soil temperature, wind direction and speed, rain gauges, and many more:

> *There is a dizzying array of factors that have an impact on or help to describe **"the weather."** The mathematics used to predict weather is referred as **chaos theory**, which is very apt! A butterfly might flick its wings in the Amazon and cause a monsoon in Bulgaria, but only if countless other factors all align perfectly. Weather predictions have won wars and lost lives and improving the quality of these predictions is a never-ending quest for a whole industry of data scientists.*

3.3 Choosing the Data to Measure

We are going to build a weather station that monitors three key weather-related parameters (factors):

Temperature: We've looked at this in detail already.

Humidity is the amount of water vapor (moisture) present in the air. Water vapor is the gaseous phase of water: tiny particles of water that are part of the air that we breath.

As with temperature, extreme levels of humidity are uncomfortable: the dry, brittle heat of the low humidity desert and the moist, cloying stickiness of the rainforest feel very different, but equally uncomfortable.

Humidity is typically measured in two ways.

1. One method is called the **specific humidity**: This is a measure of the mass of water vapor present in a kilogram mass of air (including the water). If the air is more humid, it has more water vapor. If the air is less humid, it has less water vapor.

2. A much more common measurement is **relative humidity**, which is the amount of water vapor in the air compared to the maximum amount of water vapor that the air could possibly contain at that temperature – warmer air can hold more vapor than cold air. This value is shown as a percentage.

When you watch a weather report and they mention the humidity, they are generally referring to the relative humidity: our perception of humidity correlates more with relative humidity than specific humidity.

We use a tool called a **hygrometer** to measure the amount of vapor in the air, in soil or confined spaces. There are analog and digital hygrometers: our tools will be digital.

Atmospheric (air) pressure (sometimes referred to as barometric pressure) is the amount of pressure exerted by the atmosphere:

> *Look straight up: for several miles above you there is air, lots and lots of air, and it has mass. That air is being pulled down by gravity – right onto your head! Atmospheric pressure is basically a measure of how much air there is above a given area.*

We measure atmospheric pressure by looking at the amount of pressure air exerts on a fixed area. For example, at sea level on an average day, the atmospheric pressure will be around 14.7 pounds per square inch. This amounts to

- Roughly 1 kilogram of pressure per square centimeter

- Several tons on an adult of average size

- 2100 tons on a home of about 2000 square feet

Figure 3-1 illustrates that pressure at point **X** is a factor of the weight of the air above it.

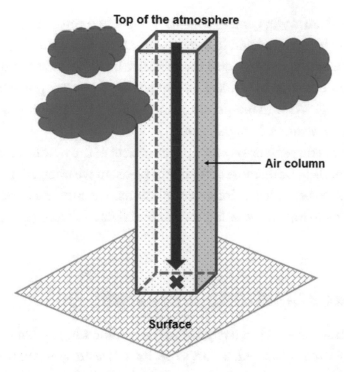

Figure 3-1. *Weight of the air in the column applying pressure to point X*

The most commonly used unit for measuring atmospheric pressure is the pascal or kilopascal: 1 kPa = 1000 Pa. Other units that are used include PSI (pounds per square inch) and millibars (or just bars). In this book we will use kPa.

To understand the kPa scale it is helpful to note that at sea level the amount of pressure is around 101kPa. As you go higher the average kPa declines – it is about 34kPa on top of Mount Everest. *The highest pressure ever recorded occurring naturally in the air at or above sea level is just below 109kPa.*

Air pressure is what makes your ears pop when you change altitude quickly and it's what we add to our tires when we pump them up. When we inflate a balloon we increase the pressure inside and many people report reactions such as headaches and anxiety when the pressure is especially high. As with temperature and humidity, atmospheric pressure is something we are able to perceive.

Atmospheric pressure is an important facet of the weather too: high pressure tends to bring more settled and pleasant weather, while dropping pressure often precedes inclement conditions. The movement of air from areas of high to low pressure is a fundamental force shaping our planet's weather.

3.4 Experimenting with Weather

An experiment is a project designed to learn something or demonstrate something already learned. In this experiment we are going to try and learn how the measures we collect correlate with the way we describe the weather:

> *This weather experiment will help us understand how temperature, humidity and atmospheric pressure relate to our perception of the weather. The experiment will show what combinations of these measures offer ideal weather conditions for the person recording the data.*

In our experiment we will collect temperature, humidity and atmospheric pressure data over an extended period and at different times. The ideal would be to keep a log over a few days.

When we take readings, we are going to make a subjective evaluation of the weather at that moment – we'll give it a score from 1 to 10, where

1. A score of 10 means it is the best possible weather for where you are at that time of year

2. A score of 1 means the worst weather it could reasonably be at this time of year

3. A score of 5 means the weather is exactly what is expected for the time of year

This is meant to be subjective: give a score based on how you feel about the weather at the moment of recording the data – don't think too hard about it! Variety is good too – try to gather results for lots of different weather conditions.

We will record the data in a table based on **Table 3-1**.

Table 3-1. *A blank data table for our weather station experiment*

Day	Time	Temperature (C)	Humidity (%)	Pressure (kPa)	Rating out of 10	Notes

This experiment mixes **objective data** (time, temperature, humidity, and pressure) with **subjective** data (rating out of 10 and notes).

> *Subjective measures are typically not very reliable and data scientists avoid them where possible, or heavily manage them where not. But we will be careful in our analysis to not extrapolate our results: this experiment will give the person who records their ratings insights into how their experience of weather is linked to temperature, humidity and atmospheric pressure. We should not expect the experiment to tell us anything else. But we will keep an open mind in our analysis.*

3.5 Building Our Weather Station Tool

To perform our experiment we need to build a digital instrument that will measure temperature, humidity and atmospheric pressure.

Figure 3-2 shows the **"circuit"** or **"block"** diagram for a digital weather station instrument.

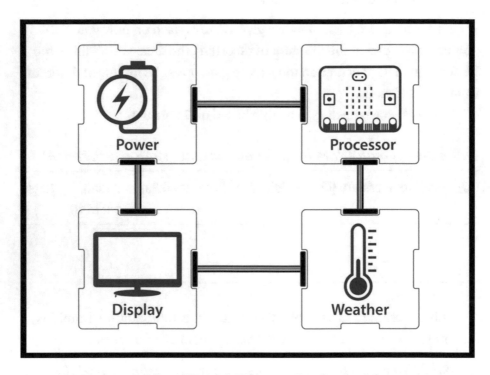

Figure 3-2. *"Circuit" or "block" diagram for the weather station tool, with a power source, weather sensor, and OLED display attached to a microprocessor*

Table 3-2 lists the hardware that we will use to build our weather station tool.

Table 3-2. *Hardware requirements for the weather station tool*

What you need	What we use	Qty	Alternatives
A microprocessor and the means to flash code onto it	micro:bit with USB cable to connect to laptop/desktop	1	Raspberry Pi Circuit Playground
Power	2xAAA battery holder	1	Seenov Inc Solar Battery
A sensor to read weather data	XinaBox SW01 – advanced weather sensor	1	SparkFun Weatherbit
A screen to view data	micro:bit 5x5 LED matrix	1	XinaBox OD01 – 64x128 OLED display
The means to connect it all together	XinaBox IM01 micro:bit bridge	1	Breadboard, edge connector breakout, crocodile/alligator leads and hookup wires
	xBus connectors to connect xChips together	3	

We will show you two options for displaying sensor data:

1. This section and **Section 3.6** show how to use the micro:bit 5x5 LED matrix.

2. In **section 3.7** we will add a 64x128 pixel OLED display to the micro:bit (the XinaBox OD01) and output our data there.

Pick the appropriate option and assemble the parts as shown in either of the following images. Alternately use a completely different set of components to build a tool that can perform the same functions. The goal is to gather data and analyze it; the tool we use is not particularly important.

Figure 3-3 shows the weather station without OLED display.

Figure 3-3. *Weather station using micro:bit LED matrix for display*

Figure 3-4 shows the weather station with OLED display.

Figure 3-4. *Weather station with OLED display*

3.6 Coding Our Weather Station

The hardware is ready, but we need to teach the microprocessor/micro:bit how to behave like a digital weather station: we need to code it.

Table 3-3 show the **natural language code** which we will convert into MakeCode blocks.

Table 3-3. *Natural language code for a digital weather station*

Step	Natural language code	Notes
1	Load any libraries that are required.	*We'll need the core micro:bit library as well as the library for our weather sensor.*
2	Keep repeating the following steps.	*The program will run continuously until the micro:bit is switched off. The following actions will be repeated…*
3	Print "T" on screen and then show the temperature.	*We just print "T" for temperature to avoid waiting ages for it to scroll.*
4	Print "H" on screen and then show the humidity.	*We just print "H" for humidity for the same reason.*
5	Print "P" on screen and then show the atmospheric pressure.	*We just print "P" for atmospheric pressure.*

No-code option: You can find a precompiled version of the code used in this section on our resource website. Go to `http://xib.one/XB` *and search for Section 3.6.*

Table 3-4 shows how to convert the **natural language code** earlier into **MakeCode** blocks that can be compiled and loaded onto your micro:bit.

Table 3-4. *Developing code with MakeCode blocks*

Step	MakeCode	Notes
1	Add the XinaBox **SW01** extension to your project.	• Click **Advanced/Extensions**. • Type in "XinaBox"[1]. • Select **SW01**.
2	Ensure you have a forever loop in your coding area.	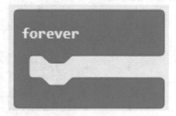
3	Add the two blocks shown here to the **forever** block: 	The first block causes "T" to be displayed. The second block displays the temperature as a whole number.
4	Add the two blocks shown here to the **forever** block after the **temperature** blocks: 	The first block causes "H" to scroll. The second block displays the relative humidity. It doesn't need to be converted to a round number.
5	Add the 2 blocks shown here to the **forever** block after the **humidity** blocks: 	The first block causes "T" to be displayed. The second block displays the pressure as a whole number.

---

[1]Alternately type in "xinabox/pxt-sw01".

Figure 3-5 shows the full **MakeCode** program listing for the micro:bit weather station.

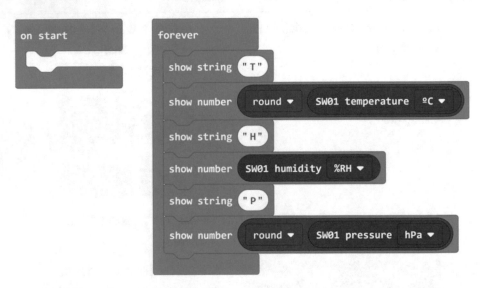

Figure 3-5. *MakeCode blocks for the micro:bit weather station*

Now that the code has been written you just need to compile it and download ("flash") it onto your micro:bit.

Once the flashing process has been completed the temperature, humidity and atmospheric pressure data will scroll continually on the 5x5 LED matrix.

The sensor readings are taken from a small chip mounted onto the SW01: the Bosch **BME280** is the tiny metal cube on the front of the SW01. Test that the sensor is working by manipulating the readings:

1. **Temperature**: Touch the sensor for a few seconds with a finger. The heat from your finger should cause the temperature to rise (**Figure 3-6**).

Figure 3-6. *Touching the sensor with a finger*

2. **Humidity**: Manipulate the humidity by breathing
   onto the BME280 sensor. The moisture in your
   breath should cause the humidity to increase
   (**Figure 3-7**).

Figure 3-7. *Humidifying the sensor*

3. **Pressure**: Take a hollow rubber tube and place
    one side on the SW01 so that it covers the BME280
    sensor. Hold the tube and board tightly together.
    Now blow air (blow hard through pursed lips) into
    the other end of the tube. This should increase the
    pressure (**Figure 3-8**).

Figure 3-8. *Applying air pressure onto the sensor*

3.7 Upgrading the Display

The micro:bit 5x5 LED matrix is adequate to display the three measurements, but with only one character on screen at once it is hard to read. And it is easy to miss a character as it scrolls across the screen.

To address this weakness, and to provide us with a larger screen on which to output data/messages, we are going to upgrade to an OLED display. We will use the 64x128 pixel OD01 display from XinaBox[2] and we will adapt the code so that we are showing all three measures on the OLED at the same time.

> ***No-code option***: *You can find a precompiled version of the code needed for this section on our **resource website** (http://xib.one/XB).*

The tool we are building here was shown earlier in **Figure 3-4**. The code for it is very similar: we just need to adapt it to direct the output to the 64x128 OLED screen instead of the micro:bit's 5x5 LED matrix.

Figure 3-9 shows the **MakeCode** blocks for micro:bit weather station with the XinaBox OD01 OLED display.

---

[2]This xChip has the SSD1306 display chip mounted onto it. This is a quite common chip used by a variety of manufacturers. Code written for the XinaBox OD01 should be relatively easy to convert for other SSD1306-based peripherals.

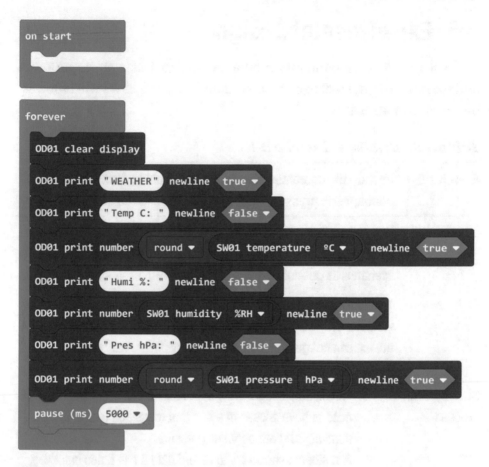

Figure 3-9. *MakeCode blocks for micro:bit weather station with OLED*

Note   This code requires the XinaBox **OD01** extension. Import this by clicking **Advanced/Extensions** and then typing in **"xinabox/ pxt-od01"**.

3.8 Experimental Design

We have all the background information needed to design our experiment and we have a digital tool to collect our data. The process we will follow is outlined in **Table 3-5**.

Table 3-5. *Details for Exercise 3-1*

Exercise 3-1	How do the combined effects of temperature, humidity, and atmospheric pressure impact on my perception of the weather
Summary	Keep a log of weather data using **Table 3-1** as a template. Data can be taken at any time of the day: aim for as many different weather scenarios as possible. Try to take around 15 measurements.
	This exercise is designed to introduce working with multiple variables and looking for patterns/correlations in the data. If the experiment goes as planned the participants may notice an intriguing correlation between temperature and pressure.
Step-by-step process	1. Participants should draw up a table to capture data. They will need to have access to a tool that measures temperature, humidity, and atmospheric pressure.
	2. Participants should try to record data a few times each day, ideally across a variety of conditions. We want to collect a broad variety of data. Exercise the caution we learned in Chapters 1 and 2 when handling the data gathering tool.
	3. When participants have collected 15 data points, that is adequate.
	4. When the data is collected work through the points listed in **Section 3.9 Analysis**.

(continued)

Table 3-5. (*continued*)

Exercise 3-1	How do the combined effects of temperature, humidity, and atmospheric pressure impact on my perception of the weather
What we will learn	• How temperature, humidity, and pressure impact on how we rate the weather.
	• An introduction to correlations.
	• Using visualizations in our analysis.
	• There is a correlation between temperature and pressure in nature[3], and there is a chance that this will be apparent in your results. If so, the visualization technique we use should help us see this.

3.9 Visualizing the Data We Collected

We have collected a fair amount of data: the completed tables are quite dense with numbers. Most people find it easier to make sense of sets of data/numbers by converting them into images such as infographics or charts. These **visualizations** are summaries of the data, and the best of them can condense years of research and data gathering into simple representations that an ordinary person can understand at a glance. In this section, we'll create a visualization on paper which we will analyze in the next section to search for answers to our original question.

Begin by drawing an empty chart on a piece of paper, as shown in **Figure 3-10**.

---

[3]Gay-Lussac's law.

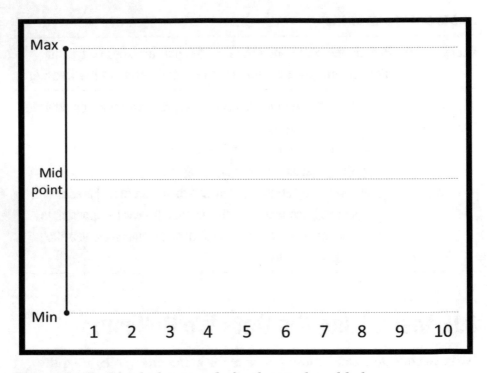

Figure 3-10. *Blank chart ready for data to be added*

Next copy the following table (**Table 3-6**) onto a separate sheet of paper and fill in the maximum and minimum values for temperature, humidity, and pressure. We are also interested in the midpoint – the value halfway between the min and the max. Fill this in by doing the following:

- Find the range by subtracting the min from the max.

- Divide the range by 2.

- Add that value to the minimum to give the midpoint.

So, if your minimum is 12 and your maximum is 20, the midpoint is 16.

For minimum 94 and maximum 101, the midpoint is 97.5.

Table 3-6. *Recording range (minimum max) weather values*

Measure	Min	Max	Range (max − min)	Half range (range/2)	Midpoint (min + half range)
Temperature	11	27	16	8	19
Humidity	30	68	38	19	49
Pressure	95	102	7	3.5	98.5

We will use Table 3-6 as a reference while we work through each row of our weather data, adding markers for temperature, humidity and pressure to the chart. We add a visually distinct marker for each variable (as shown in **Figure 3-11**).

We start with the first line of data, which is shown in **Table 3-7**.

Table 3-7. *My first data point – a miserable rainy summer day in England*

Day	Time	Temp	Humidity	Pressure	Rating	Notes
Mon	10am	16	55	97	2	Fleece & rain

When we add this line of data to the chart, it looks like **Figure 3-11**.

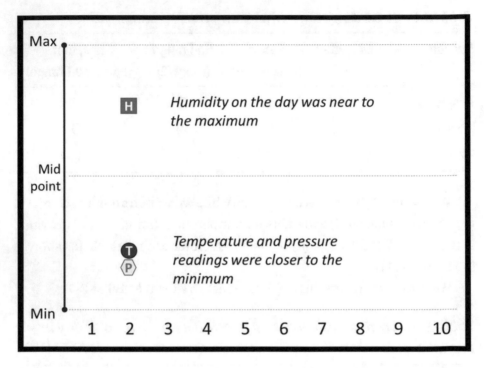

Figure 3-11. *Our chart with the first row of data added*

In **Figure 3-11** it is clear to see which value is temperature, humidity, and pressure. You can use other markers if you like, just make sure that it is easy to see which marker applies to each measure.

To place the markers on the chart, follow these steps:

- All three markers are added directly above the number 2. This is the RATING that I gave: it was cold for summer and raining heavily so I scored it a 2.

- My overall minimum temperature was 12 and my max was 27, so the midpoint is 19.5. On that day the temperature was 15, which is above the minimum but below the midpoint. *I have added my "T" marker between the minimum and the midpoint, slightly closer to the minimum.*

- My minimum humidity was 30 and my max was 68 and the midpoint was 49. The value I recorded, 58, is about halfway between the midpoint and the maximum. *I have added my "H" marker between the midpoint and maximum values.*

- My minimum pressure was 95 and the max was 101. My reading, 96, is below the midpoint (98) and above the minimum, closer to the minimum. *I have added my "P" marker just above the minimum.*

And so on: continue to use this approach and work through all the rows in the table adding markers to the chart. Some will overlap a bit, but that is OK – the idea is that we have clearly marked temperature, humidity, and pressure, so when we look at the chart, our eye can easily pick up what each mark represents. When completed your chart should look something like the one shown in **Figure 3-12**.

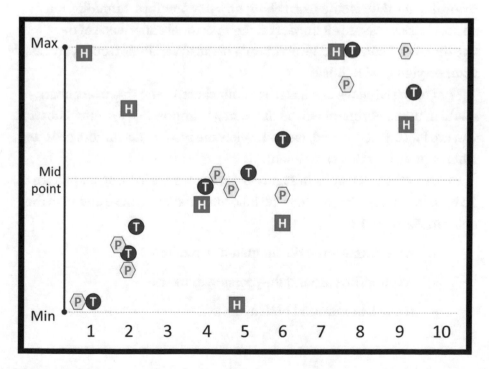

Figure 3-12. *A completed visualization*

You may have noticed that we have been a bit imprecise in how we chart our data; with a bit more effort it could have been a lot more accurate. A visualization is just a summary of the data: it is a snapshot that is easier to understand than a table full of numbers. We have taken shortcuts to make it easier and quicker to draw the chart, but if our visualization is not adequate we can always try to create it with a higher degree of accuracy. Let's see how we get on with it as it is.

3.10 Analyzing the Data We Collected

In Chapters 1 and 2 we looked at a range of different questions to ask of the data and the experimental design, and those questions should always be on your mind when data analysis begins.

But for this experiment our stated objective was very clear: the person recording the data would learn about how temperature, humidity, and atmospheric pressure all impact on their personal experience of the weather. What combined levels of each of those variables would you most want on your next holiday?

Let us see what we can learn from our chart. Given that every chart made in this experiment will be different it is impossible to anticipate what you are looking at. Instead, we will review the results the authors collected when conducting this experiment.

We saw the full results in **Figure 3-12**, but we are looking for patterns. To help in our search, consider the following marks we have added to the chart in **Figure 3-13**:

- A red box around the temperature markers

- A yellow box around the pressure markers

- A black box around both of these

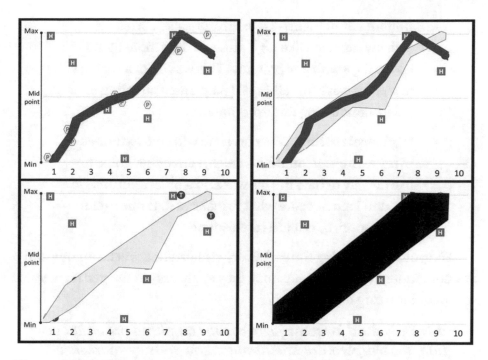

Figure 3-13. *Grouping together my temperature and pressure scores*

The black box is quite effective at showing the relationship between the rating I gave and temperature and pressure:

- **Top left of Figure 3-13**: My ratings correlate strongly with temperature: I like warm days and I tend to score them more highly compared to colder days. This is not surprising or new information: I knew this already. But it is good news: the visualization that I created shows a correlation that I know to be true, which validates the visualization we have used. Perhaps other, less obvious correlations may be lurking in the data.

- **Bottom left of Figure 3-13**: Pressure also correlates with my ratings: I like high pressure days more than I do the days with low pressure. This was bit of a surprise to me: it wasn't something I'd paid much attention to before conducting this experiment.

- **High levels of humidity correlate with the extremes of my ratings**: If humidity is high, I am either going to like the day or hate it. This was also a bit of a surprise to me, and I am not sure what to make of it. Is this useful information, or is it just interesting?

Did you find anything similar? Every visualization will be unique and any conclusions drawn are personal: they apply only to the person who recorded the rating data.

> *It is likely that, for some people who completed the visualiza-tion, the temperature and atmospheric pressure markers will show evidence of correlation. In the data shown here we can see how (relatively) low temperature and low pressure tend to occur simultaneously, as do high temperature and high pres-sure. This can be observed in Figure 3-13: the charts on the right-hand side show that pressure and temperature display very similar behavior. Did your temperature and pressure scores display this quality?*

If the answer is "yes," then the tendency might be to take it as proven that a correlation between temperature and pressure exists. But our experiment was not designed to draw this conclusion. Our experiment has met its objective: we learned a few things about how we perceive weather conditions. In addition, it has also given us a hint of something interesting: a real-world correlation between two completely different phenomena. But to be able to say with any certainty that there is a correlation between temperature and pressure we need to gather a lot more data and use more sophisticated analysis techniques. It is prudent to be cautious when drawing conclusions: hard facts are prized treasures in data science and usually are hard to come by.

3.11 Summary

In this chapter we set out to understand how temperature, humidity and pressure impact on our perception of the weather, and we have built tools and visualizations to help us answer this question. The goal was to introduce the concept of correlations and to search for some in the data we collected. We will look again at correlations in **Chapter 5**.

Some readers will have observed correlations in their visualizations which are meaningful: they tell you something that feels interesting and/ or true. Perhaps this was something you already knew (most of us know how temperature impacts on our rating of the weather) or maybe there was new information (fewer people are as aware of the impact of atmospheric pressure). The key takeout is not what we learned (or didn't learn) about temperature, humidity or pressure though. Instead, this exercise has shown that you can collect different data sets and apply analytical techniques to reveal correlations between them: using data science we can analyze the effects that different real-world phenomena have on each other. We can learn new things about the world.

CHAPTER 4

Working with Large Data Sets

In this chapter we are going to take a step forward in our data science experimentation by significantly increasing the volume of data that we collect. So far we have worked with a dozen data points, and that was adequate for our needs. But sometimes correlations (and other interesting features of data) are subtle and hard to find. The larger our data set, the more likely it is that the answers we are looking for lie within it.

If we are going to gather hundreds, thousands, or even millions of data points, there is a weakness in our toolkit: a flaw that limits how much data we can reasonably collect. Consider this question: how would we redesign the experiment in **Chapter 3** if we wanted to record the weather measures over an extended period of time, say 24 hours?

The weak spot is of course the human being with paper and pen in hand, dutifully standing in the elements for a whole day and night recording temperature, humidity and pressure every 5 minutes.

In this chapter we will begin to eliminate the human factor from the data collection process by collecting and storing the data digitally. This will allow us to build up a large collection of temperature and pressure data which we will analyze for correlations in **Chapter 5**.

P. Meitiner and P. Seneviratne, *Beginning Data Science, IoT, and AI on Single Board Computers*, https://doi.org/10.1007/978-1-4842-5766-1_4

4.1 Experimental Design

The experiment we are going to begin working on in this chapter is to investigate the correlation that we saw in **Chapter 3** between temperature and pressure. We will record these measures over a 24-hour period and then we will analyze the data and quantify the strength of the correlation. Although this sounds similar to what we did in **Chapter 3,** there are two key differences:

1. We are going to gather a lot more data.

2. We are going to use software for our data analysis.

The experiment is split over two chapters: in this chapter, we build and then use a micro:bit weather station to gather a large data set; then in **Chapter 5** we analyze that data. **Table 4-1** describes how we will go about gathering the data we need for the experiment.

Table 4-1. *Details for Exercise 4-1*

Exercise 4-1	**Is there a correlation between temperature and atmospheric pressure?**
Summary	We will gather as much temperature and pressure data as we can over a 24-hour period and then analyze it.
Step-by-step process	1. Find a suitable location for the data gathering instrument. Ensure it has fresh batteries.
	2. Place the instrument in the chosen location and power it up. It will begin recording data.
	3. After 24 hours go and collect the instrument.
	4. Extract the data from the micro:bit and load it onto a computer.
	5. Use software on your computer to undertake analysis.

(*continued*)

Table 4-1. (*continued*)

Exercise 4-1	Is there a correlation between temperature and atmospheric pressure?
What we will learn	• How to use file storage on the micro:bit. • How to construct a data file. • How to use a spreadsheet to undertake data analysis. • How correlations are quantified/measured. • How strongly temperature and pressure are correlated. • What is statistical significance.

The first thing we need for this experiment is a way of recording data over a 24-hour period.

4.2 Using the micro:bit As a File Storage Device

We can't expect a person to stand in one place for 24 hours and write down temperature and pressure readings every few minutes. To eliminate the need for this we are going to save the data we record onto file during the data collection process, and then access the file afterward. Saving data straight to file will allow us to structure our data collection process much more efficiently: we will turn on our instrument, leave it for 24 hours while data is measured and recorded, and then come back and pick it up. The file will then be retrieved.

MicroPython has a file system that allows us to save files on a micro:bit. There is no similar option on **MakeCode**, so we will need to write code for this in MicroPython.

The first step in using the file system is learning how to write data to a file. For this, all you need is a micro:bit and a power source.

The **natural language code** for writing to a file with micro:bit is listed in **Table 4-2**.

Table 4-2. *Natural language code for creating and writing to a file on the micro:bit*

Step	Description	Notes
1	Create the file.	Create a file on the micro:bit storage and provide a name for it.
2	Open the file for writing.	The file has to be "open" before it can be used.
3	Write to the file.	We will write some arbitrary data to the file, to check later that our code has succeeded.
4	Close the file.	When we are finished using a file, we should always close it.

No-code option: You can find a fully working version of the code needed for this section on our **resource website**. Go to `http://xib.one/XB` and search for **Section 4.1**.

Table 4-3 lists MicroPython code that implements the **natural language code** in **Table 4-2**.

Table 4-3. *Writing "Hello, World!" to a file with MicroPython*

Step	MicroPython
1&2	Type the following and press ENTER: `with open('hello.txt', 'w') as my_file:` This will create the file named **hello.txt** on the micro:bit storage and then open it for you to write into it later.
3	Type the following and press ENTER: `my_file.write("Hello, World!")` This will write **Hello,World!** to the file.
4	The file is closed for us – we do not need to write any code for this.

The complete **MicroPython** code for writing **"Hello, World!"** to a file is

```
with open('hello.txt', 'w') as my_file:
    my_file.write("Hello, World!")
```

Compile the code and flash it onto your micro:bit.

Once the flashing process has completed and the micro:bit resets, a file named "**hello.txt**" is created with the content you provided ("Hello, World!"). In the following sections we will show you how to view and access that file.

The code we have put onto the micro:bit basically tells it how to behave as a file storage device: we can now write anything we want to a file, including data, and we will be able to retrieve it later.

This functionality elevates the potential of the micro:bit as a tool for data science. File storage enables us to expand our data gathering capabilities and perform experiments that might otherwise not be possible. In this chapter we'll look at how to save data from the weather station to file, but the same technique could be used with any number of sensors. Your micro:bit could be the basis of digital tools that monitor all sorts of environmental measures.

4.3 Accessing Files on the micro:bit

Once you have saved data onto a file on your micro:bit the next step is to retrieve it and use it on a computer, where sophisticated analysis tools are available to us.

There are a few tools available that we can use to list and access the files stored on a micro:bit, including **Mu** and **MicroFS**. We will show you how to use Mu to access the file we have just written.

Table 4-4 presents the steps you need to follow to use **Mu** to view files on the micro:bit storage.

Table 4-4. *Listing files on the micro:bit storage with Mu*

Step	Description
1	Connect the micro:bit to your computer using a micro USB cable.
2	On the **Mu toolbar**, click the **Files** button. The **Files** pane will appear on the bottom of the Mu window. In the **Files** pane, under "**Files on your micro:bit**", you will see the list of files on your micro:bit.

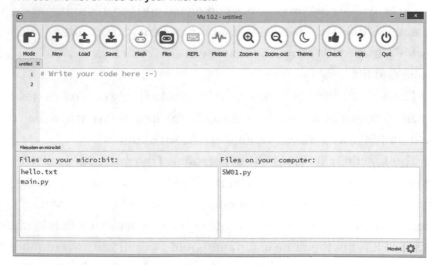

	Can you see the file you created in the preceding exercise?
3	Click the **Files** button again to close the **Files** pane.

Caution   When you flash a code onto the micro:bit using Mu a copy of your MicroPython code will save to the persistent storage (main. py). Deleting this file prevents your code from running and you need to reflash the micro:bit.

4.4 Transferring Files onto a Computer

The purpose of learning how to write data to a file is to allow us to use some of the powerful analysis tools that are available on our computers. We just need to move the file off of the micro:bit and onto our computer first. The process for doing so is outlined in Table 4-5.

Table 4-5. *Extract a file from Mu and then open it and view its contents*

Step	Description
1	On the Mu toolbar, click **Files**.
2	Drag and drop the **hello.txt** file created earlier from "**Files on your micro:bit**" to the "**Files on your computer**". The file will copy onto your computer's hard drive from the micro:bit storage and will show under "**Files from your computer**".
3	In the "**Files from your computer**" pane, right-click the **hello.txt**, and then from the shortcut menu, click **open**. The file will open with the default app installed on your computer for working with text files.
4	Inspect the file when it opens and confirm that it contains the words "Hello world!".
5	Exit from the application.

You can also access the file via whatever **File Explorer** you use on your computer. The file is saved in the same folder that Mu saves files to by default.

We have now written a file to the micro:bit memory and then extracted that file and opened it on our computer. We know everything we need to use the file system in our experiment.

4.5 Hardware Requirements

The components that our digital instrument will need to include are shown in **Figure 4-1**.

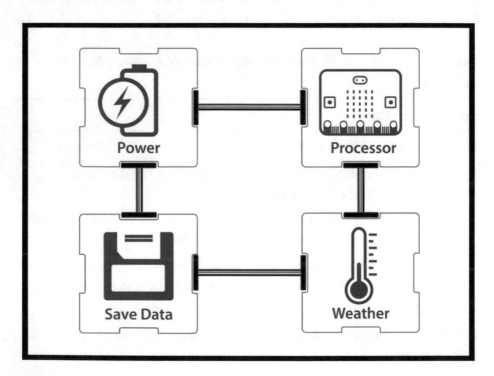

Figure 4-1. *A digital tool for reading weather data and saving it to a file*

Table 4-6 lists the specific hardware that we will use to build our weather station tool.

Table 4-6. *Hardware requirements for the weather station tool*

What you need	What we use	Qty	Alternatives
A microprocessor and the means to flash code onto it	micro:bit with micro-B USB cable to connect to laptop/desktop	1	Raspberry Pi Circuit Playground
Power	The micro:bit battery holder	1	Seenov Inc Solar Battery
A sensor to read weather data	XinaBox SW01 – advanced weather sensor	1	SparkFun Weatherbit
Persistent memory	micro:bit onboard memory	1	XinaBox IM01 micro:bit bridge (SD card)
The means to connect it all together	XinaBox IM01 micro:bit bridge	1	Breadboard, edge connector breakout, crocodile/alligator leads, and hookup wires
	xBus connectors	1	

4.6 Storing Sensor Data in a File

When we write data to a text file we can write whatever we want: any numbers or letters we like. We could store the sensor data in plain text in a format that is easily readable, like **Figure 4-2**.

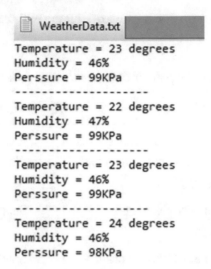

Figure 4-2. *Screen grab of a text file containing sensor data*

With this approach a lot of the file space would be taken up with the words like "Temperature", "Humidity", "Pressure", and "degrees": they help to make the file readable but they take up space in the file. Every character we write to the file "costs" us some space, and if memory is tight on the micro:bit (which it is, as we will see), we need to ditch redundant data.

The hardest decision that we have to make is to not collect humidity data: who knows what interesting observations may emerge in the analysis stage? But as you will see in the upcoming sections, the amount of memory we have on the micro:bit is very limited. Our experiment is designed to analyze the relationship between pressure and temperature, so we make the decision to omit humidity because it cannot help us answer the specific objective of the experiment. Memory space on the micro:bit file system is precious and every character we save has to earn its keep.

The core issue with the file shown in **Figure 4-2** is that it is a bespoke format that we have "invented" for this experiment. This is an unusual way to store data in a file, and it will be tricky to open it on software that has no way of recognizing the format we created. We can read it easily but computers would struggle to.

Instead we will make use of a tried and tested file format: we are going to create a **comma-separated values (or CSV) file**. Writing our data in this format will ensure that we can open the file in a spreadsheet program: the data will import automatically as a table, which will be perfect for our analysis.

CSV files have to follow a number of conventions:

- Each line of the **file** is a **record**. An end-of-line character indicates the end of a record.

- A record is a collection of **fields**: for us this means each record will include a value of temperature and pressure.

- Each value in the file is separated by a comma.

Figure 4-3 shows the same file from **Figure 4-2**, but with the data records written in CSV format.

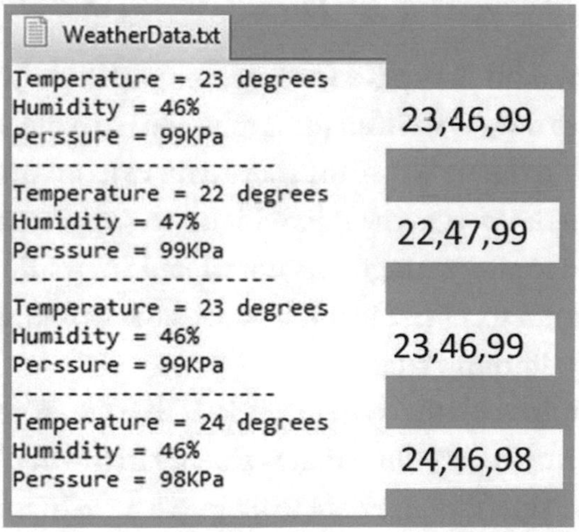

```
WeatherData.txt

Temperature = 23 degrees
Humidity = 46%                  23,46,99
Perssure = 99KPa
--------------------
Temperature = 22 degrees
Humidity = 47%                  22,47,99
Perssure = 99KPa
--------------------
Temperature = 23 degrees
Humidity = 46%                  23,46,99
Perssure = 99KPa
--------------------
Temperature = 24 degrees
Humidity = 46%                  24,46,98
Perssure = 98KPa
```

Figure 4-3. *Data file with records recorded in CSV style*

To ensure we construct our file in a CSV-valid way, when we write each record to file, we will do so as follows:

1. Start a new line in our file (or a "new record").

2. Write the temperature value to the file.

3. Write a comma to the file.

4. Write pressure to the file.

5. Write an end-of-line character.

If we follow this process, when we open our csv file in a text editor, it will look something like **Figure 4-4**.

Figure 4-4. *Data saved in CSV format viewed in a text editor*

Using the micro:bit file system presents us with another challenge. As more and more data is **written** (or **appended**) to a file, eventually the micro:bit will be unable to write any more data to it: an upper limit of file size will be reached. Despite the micro:bit having approximately **30 KB** of memory reserved for file storage, it is not capable of writing files that size in the way we want it to. Other factors, such as the working memory of the micro:bit, are also limiting factors.

The way the micro:bit file system works is that when you write anything to a file you overwrite everything that is already in the file. This means that when we want to append more data to a file, we have to read all the data already in the file into a variable, and then add the additional data we want to append to the variable. Then we write the entire contents of the file, with the new record added, back into the file. The most common limiting factor when writing data to file is the ability of the micro:bit to store the entire content of the file to a single variable.

4.7 Measuring How Many Data Points We Can Store

Our experimental design states that we should **"gather as much temperature and pressure data as we can"**. It would be helpful to know how much data we can store on a micro:bit:

- If we can store 100 data points on our micro:bit, that means we should take one reading roughly every 14 and a half minutes over a 24-hour period.

- If we can store 1000 data points on our micro:bit, that means we can take one reading roughly every 90 seconds.

- If we can store 10,000 data points on our micro:bit, that means we can take one reading roughly every 9 seconds.

To find out the capacity of the micro:bit, we will write code that will bombard it with data until it breaks, and then we'll see how much data we managed to save before it stopped working. Fun! And don't worry, the micro:bit will be fine.

We are going to write a program that fills up a file very quickly – in seconds rather than 24 hours. We will program the micro:bit to read temperature and pressure data from a SW01 and write it to a CSV file, and to continue doing so until it is no longer able to.

The **natural language code** in **Table 4-7** shows the steps we need to tell the micro:bit to follow.

Table 4-7. *Natural language code for measuring the data points*

Step	Natural language code	Notes
1	Import any libraries that are required.	We'll need the core micro:bit library as well as the library for our weather sensor.
2	Initialize our weather station.	Most sensors and add-ons for micro:bit need to be "initialized" before they can be used.
3	Stop if there is a data file already in the micro:bit storage.	If there is a data file already in the micro:bit, display "x" on the micro:bit and then exit from the code. Otherwise continue executing the code.
4	Create a file and open it for writing.	This is the file we write data to.
5	Keep repeating the following steps.	We will keep on reading and writing data until the program crashes!
6	Read the content of the file into a variable.	We can't just add data to the file – when we write anything to file, it overwrites what is already in the file. So we need to first copy the existing content of the file to a variable.
7	Read the weather sensor for temp and humidity.	We'll add ("append") the following to the variable: **temperature, humidity [new line character]**
8	Write the content of the variable back to the file.	This will write the content of the variable to persistent memory, overwriting the existing file.

No-code option: You can find a fully working version of the precompiled code used here on our **resource website**. Go to http://xib.one/XB and search for **Section 4.7**.

Note   This code requires the SW01 MicroPython library to function. Follow these steps:

1. Download the SW01 library (see the resource website).

2. Flash the precompiled code onto the micro:bit.

3. Copy the SW01 library onto the micro:bit.

Warning   Ensure that you undertake these steps in the order listed.

Table 4-8 shows how to convert the **natural language code** into **MicroPython** code that can be compiled and loaded onto your micro:bit.

Table 4-8. *Developing code with MicroPython*

Step	Description
1	Type the following:

```
from microbit import *
from SW01 import SW01
import os
import sys
```

This will import all the required libraries to your program.

| 2 | `SW01 = SW01()` |

This will initialize (or "instantiate") the SW01 library.

| 3 | `d = 0` |

```
d = 0
try:
    d = os.size("we.csv")
except:
    pass

if (d > 0):
    display.show("*")
    sys.exit()
```

When the micro:bit powers up, if there is already a file called "we.csv", then a "**x**" will display on screen and the program will stop running. This ensures we do not overwrite the file when we try to retrieve it.

| 4 | `open("we.csv", "w")` |

This will create the file named **we.csv** and open it for writing.

| 5 | `while True:` |

This is a loop (like the forever block in MakeCode): it will keep running until the micro:bit is powered down, or if there is an error (in our program it will run until the data file gets too big and causes the micro:bit to throw an error).

(continued)

Table 4-8. (*continued*)

Step	Description
| 6 | ```
try:
    with open("we.csv") as a:
        cont = a.read()
        cont = cont + str(SW01.getTempC()) + ","
        + str(SW01.getHumidity()) + "\n"

except:
    display.show(".")
    sys.exit()
``` |

This will do the following:

- Open the file for reading.
- Copy the content of the file to a variable (**cont**).
- Read temperature and humidity from the weather sensor.
- Append them as a record to the end of the content.

When the storage gets full during the writing, a **full stop** will be displayed on the LED matrix and the program will terminate.

| 7 | ```
with open("we.csv", 'w') as b:
    b.write(cont)
``` |

This will write the content of the variable **cont** to the file.

The complete **MicroPython** code listing follows:

```
from microbit import *
from SW01 import SW01
import os
import sys

SW01 = SW01()
```

```
d = 0
try:
    d = os.size("we.csv")
    except:
    pass

if (d > 0):
    display.show("*")
    sys.exit()

open("we.csv",'w')

while True:

    try:
        with open("we.csv") as a:
            cont = a.read()
            cont = cont + str(SW01.getTempC()) + "," +
            str(SW01.getHumidity()) + "\n"
    except:
        display.show(".")
        sys.exit()

    with open("we.csv", 'w') as b:
        b.write(cont)
```

When the code runs, a file will be created on the micro:bit and a new record will be continually appended to the end of the file. Follow these steps to see how many records were written before the micro:bit stopped:

Flash the code to your micro:bit. **The code will begin to run once the flashing completes**.

Wait for code to stop running, indicated by an LED as shown in **Figure 4-5**.

Figure 4-5. *The LED shown turns on to indicate that data recording has stopped*

Extract the file and open it as shown earlier.

Scroll to the end of the file and check how many rows were written – write this number down.

Repeat a few times (first delete the data file from the micro:bit storage and then restart the micro:bit). You could try different micro:bits if you have more than one, or get other people to try too. It will vary from person to person and from time to time, but it is likely you will be able to store between 50 and 60 records.

We found that it was possible to store 50 records quite reliably.

Take a look again at the code we wrote in step 3 of Table 4-8. This code prevents an existing data file from getting added to or overwritten. If your micro:bit displays a small **"x"**, that means this **"software lock"** code was activated and an existing data file was detected on the micro:bit (**Figure 4-6**). You will need to delete the file from the micro:bit file system to continue.

Figure 4-6. *The small x indicates that a data file is already in the file system*

EASY INFO CODES

x = A data file is already in the storage. No data recording happens.

.= Data recording is completed. Extract the data file from the storage.

4.8 Replicating the Weather Station Experiment with File Storage

We now have all the information and techniques we need to set up a weather station that will record 24 hours of data. We just need to choose the interval at which to record data, and our understanding of the capacity of the micro:bit comes in useful:

- We expect to be able to take 50 readings.

- In a 24-hour period, there are 86400 seconds.

- We will take a reading every 1728 seconds, which is every 28.5 minutes.

The code is almost identical to the code we wrote to test the capacity of the file storage size in **Section 4.7 (Table 4-8)**. The differences are highlighted in the following code listing.

The main difference is that in the code we wrote previously we did not want to wait between writing to the file; now we need to add in a long delay between readings. We have also added a simple feature to the code to prevent data capturing starting automatically. Now your weather station starts to capture data *ONLY* if you **press button A** on the micro:bit.

The full code is listed as follows and available on the resource website:

```
from microbit import *
from SW01 import SW01
import os
import sys

SW01 = SW01()
d = 0
try:
    d = os.size("we.csv")
except:
    pass

if (d > 0):
    display.show("*")
    sys.exit()

bp = False

while True:

    if button_a.was_pressed():
        a = open("we.csv", "w")
        bp = True

    if (bp == True):
        try:
            with open("we.csv") as a:
                cont = a.read()
                cont = cont + str(SW01.getTempC()) + "," +
                str(SW01.getHumidity()) + "\n"
        except:
            pass
            display.show(".")
```

```
with open("we.csv", 'w') as b:
    b.write(cont)
```

sleep(1440000)   # Every 28.5 minutes

When this code runs a file is created on the micro:bit. Every 28.5 minutes the weather sensor data is sampled and the values are saved in the file. If the memory buffer or storage is full the program will stop working.

The following steps explain how to use the weather station as a portable tool to capture weather data in a remote location:

1. Connect the micro:bit to your computer and flash the code onto it.

2. Remove the micro:bit from the computer and connect the portable battery power.

3. Place the micro:bit in the location that you want to capture weather data.

4. Press the button A to start capturing.

5. When the micro:bit stops (after storage gets full), an LED on the 5x5 matrix turns on.

6. Connect the micro:bit to a computer using the micro USB cable and extract the file as explained earlier.

Note   This code is designed to be as simple as possible. It can be improved in a number of ways, such as adding more error handling and providing feedback on the micro:bit LEDs as to the state of the program.

4.9 Addressing Memory Limitations

Knowing the limitations of the micro:bit file storage allows us to build our experiment accordingly. There are strategies we can employ that will ensure that we make the very best of the space available:

- Capture only the data that is needed. If you start an experiment at 1 pm and take a sensor reading every 5 minutes, you don't need to record the time whenever the sensor is read.

- You could try writing several files, perhaps write 40 records to one file and then start another before any errors occur.

- Try writing temperature data to one file and pressure data to another.

- Store the data on an SD card. It can hold more data than the micro:bit and the data on the SD card will not erase when you flash a new program to the micro:bit.

- Move the data from the micro:bit to a computer more frequently – our plan earlier involved removing the data from the micro:bit every 24 hours, but what if we could transmit the data wirelessly from the micro:bit as it's read – then storage capacity of the micro:bit would not limit us at all.

There are other ways to optimize the micro:bit persistent storage to store more data points.

- Use a short name for the sensor data file (e.g., use **we.csv** instead of **weather.csv**).

- Avoid using functions for displaying text and images on the 5X5 LED matrix (e.g., display.scroll() and display. show()).

- Avoid using additional libraries (e.g., libraries for OLED display).

4.10 Expanding Data Storage Capacity

We undertake analysis on the 50-point data set in the next chapter, and that will be more than enough data for now. But it really isn't much data at all: there are 86,400 seconds in a day, so why should we settle for only 50 data points?

One solution is to look to micro:bit add-ons to see if there are any that offer extended memory options. There are a few products available: SparkFun and XinaBox offer peripherals that are designed to expand the data logging capabilities of the micro:bit by recording data to a microSD card. If you have an XinaBox IM01 micro:bit bridge, you will notice a microSD card slot on the back.

4.11 Summary

In this chapter we learned how to use the micro:bit file system to store data as it is recorded and retrieve it later, removing the need for human involvement in the collection process. We recorded a set of weather data over a 24-hour period and that data is stored on a file, which we have transferred onto a laptop/computer.

We are now set to use the data we have collected in this chapter for some more detailed analysis, which is the focus of **Chapter 5**.

CHAPTER 5

Introduction to Data Analysis

From **Chapter 4** we have inherited a table of data. Our objective is to analyze the relationship between the temperature and pressure data we collected and see if there are similarities between these measures and, if so, are they meaningful? How can we measure the correlation?

In this chapter we will investigate how to use widely available software to answer this question, in the process unlocking a rich and easy-to-use data analysis tool that most computer users can access. Data science really is at your fingertips with the modern spreadsheet program, and this chapter will show you how to utilize these gems of technology.

5.1 Expanding Our Analysis Tools

To look at the temperature and pressure data from **Chapter 4,** we could use a similar approach to the one we used in **Chapter 3**: hand scribing a visualization. It would take a lot longer now, depending on how much data you collected, but it is possible.

This does not scale well though – what happens when we collect weather data for a whole month, or we find a way to gather (say) 10,000 data points? We will reach the stage where looking through a table to see the range, or hand drawing a chart, is no longer a task that a human being can realistically undertake.

P. Meitiner and P. Seneviratne, *Beginning Data Science, IoT, and AI on Single Board Computers*,
https://doi.org/10.1007/978-1-4842-5766-1_5

Just as we used persistent memory in **Chapter 4** to reduce the role that humans need to play in the data collection process, so too will we use digital tools to assist us in our analysis.

5.2 Software for Data Analysis

Before the adoption of computers, data analysis was very slow and labor intensive. Hand-drawn data tables similar to the ones we created in earlier chapters were used, and undertaking the sorts of data-based experiments we have been looking at required a broad skill set, lots of training, and tons of patience; a rare combination of qualities.

As computers emerged and the sorts of capabilities we've been exploring in earlier chapters were developed, so the potential for data science expanded exponentially:

Software replaced human effort, but computers and code do not replace us in the data science process. Instead they free us from the mundane tasks and allow us to dedicate our time and attention to elements of the process where human intelligence and intuition are required. Notwithstanding some recent developments in artificial intelligence (AI), no data science experiment has ever been conducted purely by computers. The human element is always present and irreplaceable.

It is fair to say that the computerization of data analysis democratized data science: powerful and usable software allows anyone with a laptop and some data to perform sophisticated analysis.

There is not a single suite of software that is the standard for data scientists. Many swear by Python, or SAS, or some flavor of SQL. In this chapter we are going to use a spreadsheet, which has all the features we need, including:

- Support for data tables. The CSV file we created will open effortlessly in any spreadsheet program.

- Many spreadsheet programs have built-in functions that we can use for data analysis, such as functions that measure correlations between two sets of data.

- Support for visualizations. Most spreadsheets allow you to easily create standard charts and other visualizations.

- Spreadsheets are relatively easy to use.

- Powerful spreadsheet programs are very widely distributed and easy to get your hands on.

- Spreadsheets are very useful in general and knowing how to use a spreadsheet program is a worthwhile skill to nurture.

5.3 Selecting a Spreadsheet Program

We are going to use Excel as our spreadsheet program, but there are other viable alternatives including Google Sheets, OpenOffice and LibreOffice.

If you use a different spreadsheet program and you are not sure if it is suitable for working through this chapter, just Google the name of your spreadsheet and the words "formula for correlation." If the software you are using comes with a built-in function for measuring correlations then you should be able to follow this chapter using that software. If not, we recommend you look at an alternative, many of which are available for free online.[1]

---

[1]On the "Cloud," which we will introduce in Chapter 6.

While we will cover the basics of using the spreadsheet program for data analysis, there are a few core skills you will need which we will not cover in this book. You need to know how to:

- Open the spreadsheet program and start a new project.

- Open a CSV file in the spreadsheet program.

- Type values into cells.

- Navigate around the spreadsheet.

Figure 5-1 outlines some key terms we use to describe different aspects of a spreadsheet.

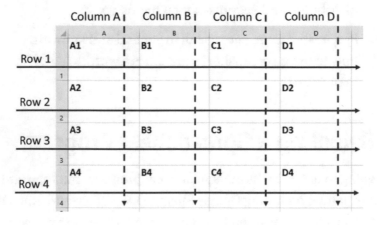

Figure 5-1. *Naming conventions for columns, rows, and cells*

- **Rows**: Rows run laterally, left to right. and are numbered from 1, 2, 3 and so on.

- **Columns**: Columns run vertically, top to bottom, and are labeled A, B, C and so on.

- **Cells**: A cell is the place where a column and a row intersect, and they are labeled according to their column and row: A1 or B3 or C8, for example.

5.4 Measuring Correlation

In **Chapter 3** we saw that temperature and pressure behaved in a similar way: they appeared to be related somehow and we used the term **"correlation"** to describe this relationship. We were unable to say how strong this correlation was though – we don't have the language to describe this in an objective way. Are they 100% corrclated, or 0.5 correlated, and do either of these questions actually mean anything?

Correlation coefficients are measured on a scale from -1 to +1:

- The strongest possible correlation between two data sets gets a score of 1. When two data sets have a correlation score of 1, it usually means that they are both describing exactly the same thing (e.g., temperature in Celsius and temperature in Fahrenheit will have a correlation of 1).

- A score of 0 or very close to 0 means there is no relationship between the two sets of numbers. The things they measure are completely unrelated.

- Two sets of a couple of hundred random numbers are unlikely to have a correlation score of exactly 0. We might expect the score to be around 0.1, or -0.1, but as they are random, anything can happen.

- There is no "good" or "bad" correlation score – it is just a description of how similarly two data sets behave.

How would you interpret a correlation score of -1?

Table 5-1 provides a simple exercise that demonstrates the correlation scores between sets of numbers.

Table 5-1. *Investigating correlation coefficients*

Step	What to do	Notes
1	Open the spreadsheet program and start a new project/ spreadsheet/workbook.	Start with a blank sheet – we will type in some numbers.
2	In Column A: Type the numbers 1 to 100.	There are tricks to help you do this: you don't need to type out each number.
3	In Column B: Copy the numbers from the first column.	Column A and Column B are identical – so they should have a maximum correlation score.
4	In Column C: Type the numbers 100 to 1, so they count down in each cell.	This is the reverse of Column A. How will this correlate with column A?
5	In Column D: Type in the numbers 2, 4, 6… to 100 and then go backward: 98, 96, 94, etc.	In this column the numbers are very similar to Column A until the middle, when they start declining. How do we expect column D to correlate Column A?
6	In Column E: Enter random numbers between 1 and 100 in each of the 100 cells.	Use a random number generating function. For both Excel and Google Sheets, you can use: = 100*RAND()
7	In Column F: Copy what you did in column 5.	Columns E and F both have just random numbers throughout.

Once complete your spreadsheet should look something like
Figure 5-2.

◢	A	B	C	D	E	F
1	1	1	100	2	17.10145	27.83091
2	2	2	99	4	43.88679	16.26478
3	3	3	98	6	63.31731	40.043
4	4	4	97	8	80.78086	58.99108
5	5	5	96	10	30.96587	25.14073
6	6	6	95	12	18.37345	29.61452
7	7	7	94	14	68.74148	62.17132
8	8	8	93	16	89.41478	77.62148
9	9	9	92	18	10.51281	43.3196
10	10	10	91	20	63.549	84.49571
11	11	11	90	22	86.34147	76.4262
12	12	12	89	24	24.33936	8.803535
13	13	13	88	26	47.99066	65.41375
14	14	14	87	28	86.34912	14.29891
15	15	15	86	30	60.42123	72.41918
16	16	16	85	32	0.383978	6.688083

Figure 5-2. *The top of a spreadsheet filled in as per Table 5-1*

It is worth taking a pause here and pondering the questions raised in
the Notes column in **Table 5-1**. What are your expectations? Once you
have set your expectations, work through the steps in **Table 5-2** to calculate
correlation scores.

5.5 Calculating Correlation Scores

Follow the steps in **Table 5-2** to find out the correlation scores when
comparing the different columns we created in **Table 5-1**.

Table 5-2. *Adding correlation scores to Table 5-1 data*

Step	What to do	Notes
1	Use the same spreadsheet created in Table 5-1.	We are going to type labels in Column G and formulae into column H.
2	Search online for details of how to use the correlation function in your spreadsheet program.	For both Excel and Google Sheets, the formula for the correlation score of 2 columns of data is =CORREL(A1:A100,B1:B100)
3	In cell G1, type **Correlation of A and B** In H1 type in =CORREL(A1:A100,B1:B100)	This compares the data in Column A with the data in Column B. Once you have entered the formula, you will see the result. Is it what you expected?
4	In cell G2, type **Correlation of A and C** In H2 type in =CORREL(A1:A100,C1:C100)	This compares the data in Column A with Column C. Once you have entered the formula, you will see the result. Is it what you expected?
5	In cell G3, type **Correlation of A and D** In H3 type in: =CORREL(A1:A100,D1:D100)	This compares the data in Column A with the data in Column D. Once you have entered the formula, you will see the result. Is it what you expected?
6	In cell G4, type **Correlation of A and E** In H4 type in: =CORREL(A1:A100,E1:E100)	This compares the data in Column A with the data in Column E. Refresh the random numbers and see how the correlation score changes when you do.

(continued)

Table 5-2. (*continued*)

Step	What to do	Notes
7	In cell G5, type **Correlation of E and F** In H5 type in: =CORREL(E1:E100,F1:F100)	Columns E and F both contain random numbers – does Column E correlate more strongly with Column A or Column F? And does this change when you refresh the random numbers?
8	Try comparing other columns together to see their correlation scores.	It is fun to use the formulae in a spreadsheet to come up with columns of numbers with different correlation scores.
9	Save and close.	We will not use this spreadsheet again.

We can learn a few things about correlation coefficients from these results:

- Column A and Column B are identical. Their correlation score is 1.

- Column A and Column C are completely the opposite: When one goes up, the other goes down – they are basically a mirror image of each other. But the behavior of one is completely predictable by looking at the other. Their correlation score is -1.

Figure 5-3 shows an experiment where a correlation of -1 might be measured. The height of the green ball and the height of the blue ball have a perfect negative correlation.

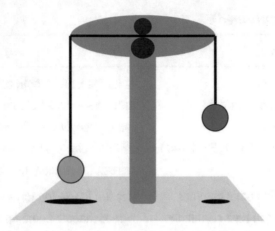

Figure 5-3. *As the blue ball ascends so the green ball descends*

- Although Columns A and D behave similarly at first, this does not last the full data set. Their behavior is not related and knowing that one column is ascending does not help us guess whether the other is ascending or descending. There is a very low correlation score (-0.03).[2]

Figure 5-4 shows the values of **Columns A** and **D** on a line chart.

---

[2]Imagine if we had only looked at the first 50 rows. At that point the two columns were highly correlated, but by the time we reached 100, the pattern had changed. Perhaps if we went to 150 rows the correlation score would change again? What about 175, or 200?

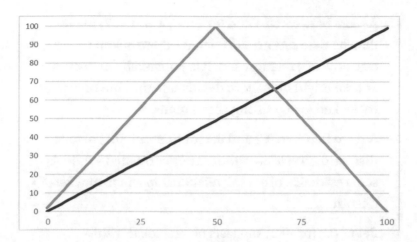

Figure 5-4. *A line graph showing values from Column A to Column D*

5.6 Understanding a Correlation Coefficient/Score

We've seen what a correlation of 1, -1, and close to 0 means, but what should we make of two sets of data that have a correlation of 0.4, or -0.5, or 0.78? There are no hard-and-fast rules and context is always a factor, but outside of very tightly controlled experiment the following guidelines can be used to interpret a correlation score:

- Where two data sets have a correlation of 0.7 of more (or -0.7 or less), then it is safe to describe it as a **strong** correlation. Above 0.9 would be very strong. If we see scores this high in our data science experimentation, we would be extremely interested to understand the underlying relationship between the things being measured.

- A score between 0.4 and 0.7 (or -0.4 and -0.7) means that the data sets are correlated – there is some evidence of a relationship. It is potentially interesting and we might look more deeply into this, but only after we looked at any strong correlations.

- A score between 0.2 and 0.4 (or -0.2 and -0.4) means that the data sets are **moderately** correlated – there is some evidence of a weak relationship which may be of interest.

- Below 0.2 (or -0.2) suggests no real relationship between the data sets at all.

Correlations do not have to be strong to be useful results: discounting correlations between data sets might be the objective of an experiment. For example, your experiment might set out to show that height and hair color are not linked. A close-to-zero correlation score would help to demonstrate this.

5.7 Calculating the Correlation Score for Weather Data

The process of calculating the strength of the correlation between our temperature and pressure data is quite straightforward now, and is detailed in **Table 5-3**.

Table 5-3. *Calculating the correlation coefficient for our temperature and pressure data*

Step	What to do	Notes
1	Open the CSV file from Chapter 4 in your spreadsheet program.	It should import as 2 columns, with headers. Check the data has imported correctly; if not, try again or Google a quick fix.
2	In D1 type in: **Correlation score =** In E1 type in: =CORREL(A1:A42,B1:B42)	Adapt the formula depending on how many rows of data there are. Note the answer.
3	Save the file.	We will use it later.

The formula that we typed in **C1** should return a number between -1 and 1: this is a measure of the extent to which the temperature and pressure readings you took during your experiment are correlated. Whatever score you got has answered the question posed in our experiment[3]: is there a correlation between temperature and pressure? Use the guidelines from **Section 5.5** to uniquely answer this question.

In our experiment we were constrained in how much data we could collect, which meant we only looked at temperature and pressure. With more data at our disposal, analysis of correlation scores can have some great applications:

---

[3]It is likely that you recorded a strong or moderately strong correlation. This is explained by Gay-Lussac's law, also known as the pressure-temperature law: all other things being equal, if the temperature of a volume of air increases the, pressure increases, and vice versa.

- We saw in Chapter 1 that there are a large number of data points that we can measure that relate to the weather – dozens of them. Over many years climate scientists have analyzed these and measured correlations between them. This has helped build up a body of knowledge about the weather that is used, among other things, to make predictions.

- Medical science is built on the humble correlation. Where there is a strong correlation between a new procedure and the life expectancy of a patient, we might say a "cure" has been found.

- Imagine being able to measure 100 things about yourself and then finding the 5 that most correlate with your happiness.

5.8 Using Other Analysis Functions

There is a lot more to data analysis than just looking for correlations, and most spreadsheet programs provide a broad range of functions you can use.

Complete the exercise in **Table 5-4** to answer these questions:

- What were the highest and lowest temperature and pressure scores?

- What was the mean average temperature and pressure during the period?

- What single reading was most common for temperature and pressure?

Table 5-4. *Using key statistical functions in a spreadsheet*

Step	What to do	Notes
1	Open the file from **Table 5-3** in your spreadsheet program.	We are going to find out some more information about our temperature and pressure data.
2	Type in the following in the cells indicated: D2: Maximum pressure = D3: Minimum pressure = D4: Range of pressure = D5: Average pressure = D6: Modal pressure = D7: Maximum temperature = D8: Minimum temperature = D9: Range of temperature = D10: Average temperature = D11: Modal temperature =	These are labels: we type them in to help us keep track of things. We will type in formulae next to them, corresponding to the labels.
3	Type in the following: E2: =MAX(B1:B42) E7: =MAX(A1:A42)	Find the maximum temperature and pressure.
4	Type in the following: E3: =MIN(B1:B42) E8: =MIN(A1:A42)	Find the minimum temperature and pressure.
5	Type in the following: E4: =D2-D3 E9: =D7-D8	Subtract the minimum from the maximum to give you the range.

(continued)

Table 5-4. (*continued*)

Step	What to do	Notes
6	Type in the following: E3: =AVERAGE(B1:B42) E8: =AVERAGE(A1:A42)	Find the average temperature and pressure.
7	Type in the following: E3: =MODE(B1:B42) E8: =MODE(A1:A42)	Find the modal temperature and pressure. This is the most common value – the value that is repeated the most times.
8	Save your work.	We will use this spreadsheet to help create visualizations in the next section.

5.9 Using Visualization Tools

Most spreadsheet programs provide you with tools to generate visualizations, and these usually include some standard chart types (e.g., line, bar, and pie charts). Across the different programs the way you generate and edit charts is similar, and online support is generally good. We will generate a very simple line chart showing our temperature and humidity data using the following steps, which you should be able to follow in whichever spreadsheet program you are using:

1. Highlight both columns of data in the spreadsheet.

2. Click **insert**.

3. Find the **chart** option and click that.

4. Select the first **line chart** option listed.

This should give you a rudimentary line chart, which may be good enough for your needs. You can edit the chart in a number of ways which differ from program to program, but if you follow these simple guidelines, you should be fine:

- To select a specific part of a chart, click it. Usually some kind of visual guide (e.g., markers around the corners) will show you what you have selected.

- If you want to edit something on the chart, select it and then right-click. Look for an option with the word **edit**. Click it.

- Play around with settings – you can't break anything.

- Start again if you don't like what you have.

Our chart is shown in **Figure 5-5**. We've omitted the time of day; it would usually be shown along the bottom on the x axis. See if you can guess when dawn broke by looking at the data.

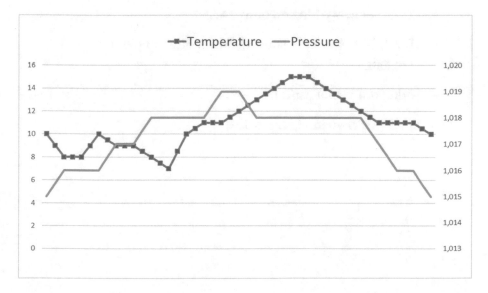

Figure 5-5. *A line chart showing temperature and pressure over 24 hours. Taken in the United Kingdom in September 2019*

5.10 Reporting

Our analysis of the temperature and pressure data has yielded a number of outputs. We have a correlation score, max, min, range, average and a visualization. But our experiment is not complete until the results have been written up and a report has been delivered to our **stake holders**. These are the people on whose behalf we are undertaking our data science experiment – perhaps our employers, or a charitable foundation, or an investor. Even if we are doing it for ourselves, a blog or social media update is still a form of reporting.

The way in which you put together this report will depend on the software that you use, but however you do so there are a number of guidelines that are useful to try and follow:

- Include a brief summary of what your experiment was.

- Show the sample size – how many data points you collected.

- Try to fit everything on one page.

- Don't be technical – show results written in plain English.

- Add your visualization.

Our report is shown in **Figure 5-6.**

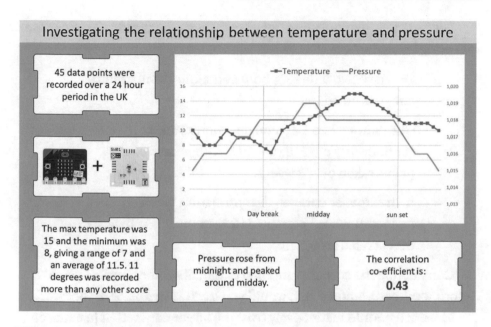

Figure 5-6. *A one-page report showing an overview of the experiment*

5.11 Statistical Significance

Consider the examples we looked at in **Table 5-1** and **Table 5-2**. We copied out a couple of columns containing 100 numbers and then we checked the correlation coefficients between different columns. Have a look again at Column A and Column D, as well as **Figure 5-4**.

Do you think the results would have been the same if we only used the first 50 numbers of both columns?

Let's ask a similar question but phrased very differently. Consider the following scenario:

- You have two data sets, both containing temperature and pressure data.

- One data set has 1 million data points taken continuously over 10 years. The other has 500 data points taken over 2 weeks.

- In the smaller data set, the correlation between temperature and pressure is 0.5. In the larger data set, the correlation is 0.75.

Considering the scenario outlined earlier, if someone asked you to describe the correlation score, would you say it is **strong** or **moderate**?

Most of us would instinctively trust the larger data set – it just makes sense that 10 million data points contain more substance, more potential information, than 1000 data points. Each data point contains some value – it is like a pixel, making up an image. Having more data points is like having more pixels: as the resolution improves so does our ability to see the big picture.

Logic therefore tells us that results coming from larger data sets are somehow more meaningful than results coming from a smaller set. Similarly, it is logical to say that results coming from large, valid, and reliable data sets are more meaningful than results coming from less **rich** data. The term "rich" data is very apt – it is used to refer to data that has the potential to yield lots of information.

The concept of **statistical significance** is the best measure of how meaningful a specific result is. The mathematics of calculating significance is quite complex and not in scope for us here, but very interesting and well worth looking into. The important thing for a data scientist is not knowing the mathematics that significance scores are built on though, it is understanding what a statistical significance score means:

- A correlation coefficient is completely different from a significance score.

- Significance is usually shown as a percentage or an index.

- It is frequently referred to as the **confidence** level.

- It is a measure of the extent to which a specific result is likely to recur if the experiment is repeated.

- If a result has a significance score of 50%, that means that if the experiment were to be repeated there is a 50% chance that the same result would be observed. The result is true half the time and not true the rest of the time.

- If a result scored 100% significance, then that means it is always true – an unassailable fact. Scores of 100% are very rare.

- Data scientists set an arbitrary threshold: a significance level above which a result can be considered a "fact" – usually 95% or 99%. Pretty much every scientific fact that we have ever been presented with has been demonstrated in an experiment where the significance score was greater than 95% or even 99%, but almost always lower than 100%.

As a rule of thumb, it is rare to find significant results in a data set with less than 50 readings; larger data sets are more likely to yield significant results, and the more valid and reliable data is, the more likely significant results will be uncovered. In most data science experiments, results that are not significant are discarded or treated with caution.

It is possible to calculate the significance of a correlation score, and readers are encouraged to look more deeply into this.

5.12 Summary

In this chapter we have looked at how to use a spreadsheet to help us undertake analysis of a data table we built in **Chapter 4**. The key challenge we solved was extracting the data from the micro:bit and getting it into a tool that is better suited to the task of data analysis. Spreadsheets are powerful and widely available, but why stop at moving data from the micro:bit to a laptop when the Internet of Things is just a modem away.

CHAPTER 6

Introducing IoT to Data Science

In this chapter we will look at the **Internet of Things** (IoT) from the perspective of data scientists. What is IoT and how can it help us expand our data science capabilities?

6.1 The Weakness in Our Data Science Toolkit

In the preceding chapters we have undertaken increasingly complex data science experiments. Our questions and our tools have grown more sophisticated, but the underlying process typically includes the following steps:

1. **Curiosity**: The process always starts with curiosity; a question.

2. **Experimental design**: We then work out how we are going to answer this question – what data should we gather and what tools do we need? We define the steps that are going to be taken to execute our experiment.

© Philip Meitiner, Pradeeka Seneviratne 2020
P. Meitiner and P. Seneviratne, *Beginning Data Science, IoT, and AI on Single Board Computers*,
https://doi.org/10.1007/978-1-4842-5766-1_6

3. **Data collection**: The experiment involves a period of collecting data.

4. **Data transference**: Data that has been collected is moved off of the data gathering tool into some other environment more conducive to analysis. So far we have transcribed data onto paper and saved data onto file.

5. **Analysis**: The data that has been retrieved from our data gathering tool is analyzed using appropriate techniques and software.

6. **Reporting**: We have developed visualizations and seen how data can be presented as conversational facts.

7. **Introspection**: Deriving learnings from the experiment to improve future designs.

The greatest weakness so far in our data science toolkit is in step 4. We have written data down on a piece of paper and used the micro:bit's persistent memory to record data, but neither of these solutions can scale very well. To collect much greater volumes of data we are going to need to find other ways to transfer data off of our micro:bit-based data collection tools and into our analysis software. It is here that IoT will prove its value to us.

6.2 Internet of Things Overview

Before we can find a role for IoT in our data science experiments we need to have a clear and simple understanding of what IoT actually is. And not a technical understanding; there are other books for that. We need to understand how IoT can be useful to us in our data science work; then we'll learn how to utilize it.

To understand the Internet of Things it helps to first consider the "Internet of Everything" and the "Internet of Humans."[1] **Figure 6-1** shows all the computers in the world that are connected to each other: the Internet of Everything.

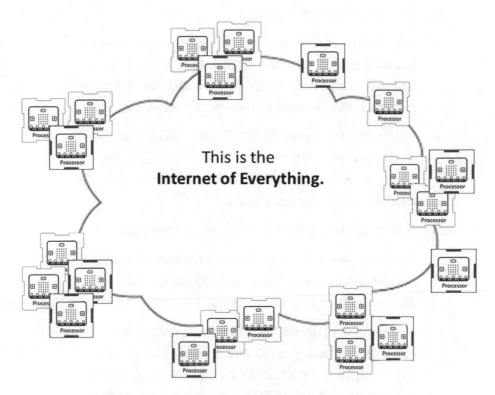

Figure 6-1. *The Internet of Everything: all the connected computers in the world*

In **Figure 6-1** the blocks highlighted in red represent the computers and smart devices that humans use to access Facebook, YouTube, email, online banking, and so on. This is the "Internet of Humans": all of our experiences on a browser or a connected app occur on these devices.

---

[1]This is a made-up phrase not used outside this book, but it makes sense and is useful in this chapter.

The smart devices that make up the Internet of Things are all the blocks that are not highlighted in red in **Figure 6-1**. These devices go about their business and interact with each other without any need for direct human intervention.

The IoH and IoT are very similar:

- The Internet of Humans (IoH) is built so that **people** can understand it: data is presented to us in a way that we find easy to digest and, where we are required to interact with the IoH, it is usually made quite easy for us.

- The Internet of Things (IoT) is built in a way that **machines** can easily understand it: it is designed to allow data to be moved around from one place to another quickly and efficiently.

The IoH and IoT are not distinct and separate systems:

- There isn't separate infrastructure for the IoH and IoT: just like trucks and cars drive on the same roads, so data for both travels over the same networks.

- There is a lot of overlap: the IoH uses services and accesses data from the IoT and is used by humans to control and calibrate the IoT. In some respects the IoH is the "front end" of the IoT: it is a window through which we see and interact with the IoT.

There are protocols[2] and technologies that are distinct to IoT and IoH. Extending the motoring analogy used earlier, these differences might be compared to those between a diesel and a petrol vehicle.

---

[2]To drive a car from one place to another, we don't need to know much about how the engine works. Similarly we are learning how to use IoT in data science, not how to be an IoT developer or engineer. This book avoids technical details that

So, an IoT system is one where there is interaction between two or more machines using the Internet, and where there is no human being involved at any stage in the process.

But why would fridges, or houses, or satellites want to share data, and why would they do so without involving humans? All sorts of innovative and practical applications have been developed, and more and more are being imagined and built:

- Smart houses. A lot of homes use heating and lighting, which consume energy and cost money. Sensors placed around a home can provide information about which parts of the home need to be lit or heated, and a central control unit can adjust the levels accordingly.

- Smart streetlights are becoming more and more common. Not only do they help cut down on unnecessary use of lighting, they are often integrated with monitors that report other data – environmental sensors or CCTV cameras are often used.

- IoT-enabled health monitors send medical data to AI systems that analyze it and send out alerts if any concerning data is observed.

- Some buildings have IoT-enabled monitors that record data pertaining to the state of the building. If data suggests the building needs maintenance, then details will be sent to an engineering team who will come in and undertake an inspection.

One theme that emerges from the preceding examples is that the IoT serves us: it is typical for IoT systems to collect and analyze data and

---

do not contribute to our data science journey, and this most definitely includes Internet data transfer protocols.

then to perform an action that is of benefit to people. It may alert us when undesirable conditions are identified, or it may adjust a system to make it less dangerous or more efficient.

IoT is not the means by which computers take over the world; instead, it is how we as humans have delegated great swathes of activity to computers to make our own lives easier and more comfortable. For now, at least, computers dance to the tune of humans.

6.3 Anatomy of the Cloud

Before we look at how to incorporate IoT into our data science journey, there are a few remaining concepts that we will encounter and which we need to have a basic understanding of. In this section we will clarify some semantics and look at the different components that make up an IoT system.

Firstly, expanding on **Section 6.2**, we will look at definitions of the Internet, the Internet of Things, and "the cloud":

- The **Internet.** In **Section 6.2** we referred to the Internet of Everything and the Internet of Humans, but we failed to identify whether either of these is what is meant by the phrase: "the Internet." Most people would equate the Internet with "the Internet of Everything."

- The **cloud** is a subset of the Internet of Everything: it is made up of a number of computers, often powerful servers, that provide services to other computers on the Internet. They might save data, or process it, or perform transactions, or even provide artificial intelligence (AI) services.

- The **Internet of Things** can be thought of as the systems within the Internet where data is transferred or processed without human intervention.

Figure 6-2 shows a simplified view of how different connected components fit together.

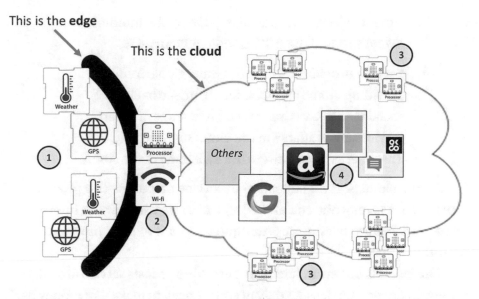

Figure 6-2. *The anatomy of an IoT system*

Referring to the numbered elements in **Figure 6-2**:

1. **Edge devices**: Some digital devices are connected to the real world, such as sensors that record weather data or provide GPS coordinates. When they are connected to the Internet they provide new data from outside of it. So these devices are at the edge of the IoT and we call them edge devices.

2. **Gateway devices**: A gateway device provides an edge device with the means of connecting to the Internet/IoT. Bear in mind that if you want to connect an edge device to the IoT, then it suggests that you want to send data somewhere – to some other device. There are two main options (3 and 4 below).

3. Other devices/networks that make up the Internet of Everything and the IoT (as seen in **Figure 6-1**).

4. **Service providers**: There is a huge global industry providing online services. Email, image backup, social media, banking, and a huge range of other services are available in the cloud for us to use. These services constitute the backbone of the cloud.

So, the cloud is a vast collection of service providers who provide tools (such as email and social media) which we use over the Internet. These services are not free; for example it costs Google to provide and maintain Gmail.

The cloud is not an altruistic undertaking. It costs service providers money to provide services, so they of course need to make that money back.

In some way each gateway into the cloud needs to pay a price to access the services they use on the cloud. We may pay by providing a cash payment for a specific service, or by providing data about ourselves that is of value to a service provider. Often they may make their money by enabling advertisers to reach us with marketing messages.

It is true that some services are genuinely free, but just like when you enter a shop you expect to pay for any item you walk out with, so should you expect to pay, in some form or another, when using cloud services.

In this book we'll use free services to get started with the IoT – most providers offer free trial periods. But they are always limited in various ways, and to use these services on an unlimited basis it will be ultimately necessary to pay a fee.

6.4 Transferring Data from a micro:bit

In **Section 6.1** we looked at the different aspects of the data science process and we identified the greatest weakness in our existing tool set: we are unable to use the micro:bit to collect any real volume of data. It is great at measuring the data that we need, just not very suitable when it comes to storing it.

IoT offers us a solution for this: it provides the means to go from recording a few dozen data points to a virtually unlimited number:

By transferring the data as soon as it is recorded we avoid the limitations inherent in storing the data on the micro:bit. If we could move the data to another platform that is more suited to storing large amounts of data then we are limited by that platform, rather than the micro:bit. There are IoT platforms that are designed to make it easy to do just this: they provide cloud services to store data. So, if we can find a way to transfer our data to a suitable IoT platform, then the micro:bit's data storage issues cease to be a limiting factor on our data science capacity.

The challenge we face is: how can we transfer data as it is being collected on the micro:bit to another device? There are four ways this could be done:

1. By having a person transcribe data as it is recorded, then enter it manually onto the next device. We tried this sort of thing in earlier chapters and abandoned it quite quickly as it was too labor intensive. This is not a viable option.

2. By connecting a peripheral that can store volumes of data. At the end of Chapter 5, we looked at an SD card solution for the micro:bit that allows for data files in excess of 1 gigabyte to be stored. This is an excellent solution if you have access to the hardware

and if you don't mind only being able to access the data later, after it has been collected.

3. By using a cable to join the micro:bit and the other device. We'll look at **wired** options in **Section 6-6**.

4. By using a **wireless** option. Computers are able to transmit data wirelessly in a number of ways, which we look at in **Section 6-5**.

We have set our sights on transferring the data from our micro:bit to the cloud[3] where a broad range of tools and capabilities will enable us to significantly increase out data science productivity. We will now consider options 3 and 4 and decide on which to pursue in later chapters.

6.5 Wireless Communication Options for IoT

Wireless communication is not new: our ancestors used it long before the age of computing, and not just to talk to each other. Signal fires and lighthouses are wireless communication methods that utilize light waves to send a message.

There are a lot of similarities in how people and computers communicate wirelessly:

---

[3]A more technically correct way of saying this using the terminology introduced in Section 6.3 would be: "we have set our sights on making the micro:bit an IoT edge device by connecting it to a gateway, which we will use to send data to a cloud based service."

- People can transmit and receive data wirelessly very easily and frequently. Speaking is the most obvious way, but other factors such as body language are used to communicate data to people who are in a vicinity to hear or notice us.

- Computers can transmit and receive data wirelessly very easily and frequently. Transmitting radio waves is the most common way, but other options are available. We will not pay these any attention.

There are three leading technologies that transmit and receive radio signals to communicate data and which are used to connect devices to the Internet/IoT and to access cloud-based services:

- **Bluetooth**: The micro:bit has a built-in radio transmitter that conforms to the BLE (Bluetooth Low Energy) specification. The radio functionality can be used on its own, without invoking the Bluetooth protocol. We will explore the capabilities of Bluetooth in **Chapter 7**, and then in **Chapter 8** we will look at how the radio can be used without Bluetooth.

- **Wi-Fi: Chapter 9** explains a bit more about Wi-Fi and shows how to add Wi-Fi capabilities to your micro:bit.

- **LoRaWAN** and **Sigfox**: LoRaWAN (Long Range Wide Area Network) and Sigfox. These are both exciting and growing technologies, but they currently have limited support on the micro:bit. Bluetooth, radio, and Wi-Fi are much better supported and will be suitable for a wide range of data science applications. It is these wireless communication methods that we will use in the remainder of this book.

> **Note**   There are circumstances where LoRaWAN or Sigfox are more appropriate technologies than Bluetooth or Wi-Fi. The range on LoRa and its low power model make it very suitable for deploying remote sensors: it is a popular choice in high-altitude experimentation, such as communicating data from sensors on a weather balloon. In the interests of limited space, we are omitting these technologies from this book.

6.6 Transmitting Data Using a Serial Connection

A UART (USB) cable can be used to extract data from a micro:bit. Data can be transferred over a "serial" cable from a micro:bit directly to a computer, where it can be saved in great volume (**Figure 6-3**).

Figure 6-3. *A micro:bit attached to a computer using a USB cable can transmit data over that cable to the computer*

This approach is tried and tested, but it does have some limits:

- The measuring instrument has to be a cable-length away from the computer. There will be a number of data science use cases where this sort of solution will do adequately, but we are going to use the remainder of this book to look at wireless solutions: ways that we can transmit data between the micro:bit and another device without the constraint of a physical connection.

- The process is not trivial. There are code libraries and apps that make it as simple as possible, but the range of options and configuration can make it a bit tricky for beginners.

- It is without doubt a useful tool to have in your repertoire, but there are no use cases it will enable that the wireless options we explore later in the book cannot do just as well.

If a cabled solution will suit all of your needs, you should consider looking into this, and the Micro:bit Foundation's website has all the details you will need.

Note   There is a relatively new cabled solution available for micro:bit that is much easier to use than the methods currently promoted by the Micro:bit Foundation and the community. The **Excel Data Streamer** app is available on the latest version of Excel and can be used to feed data from the micro:bit (or any edge device) directly into Excel (via a serial/ USB port). Given the ease with which Excel can be integrated with other Office 365 applications, this solution is potentially very powerful. If you have access to Office 365 and are looking for a cabled solution, then you should consider this.

6.7 Summary

In this chapter we have tried to demystify some of the terminology associated with the IoT and look at the technology that it is built upon. We have seen how it can help us address the main weakness in our toolkit: data storage limitations. There are also hints that it can offer us other benefits: if cloud computing provides services that we can access, surely some of those services will be useful in our data science endeavors? We have learned that wireless communication is the ideal way to connect to the IoT, and using Bluetooth, radio, or Wi-Fi, we will build a gateway to connect our edge devices to the cloud, thereby solving the problem of data storage. We will then be in a position to investigate what else IoT has to offer.

CHAPTER 7

Using Bluetooth for Data Science

In the lead up to this chapter we have looked at how the BBC micro:bit can be used to build data gathering tools that enable us to undertake meaningful real-world data science experiments. In the process we have identified a flaw in our capabilities: the micro:bit can measure almost unlimited volumes of data, but saving that data and/or getting it off of the micro:bit (and into an environment where we can use it) has been challenging.

At the end of **Chapter 6** we concluded that wireless technology could provide us with the means to extract data as it is recorded. In this chapter we will look at one of the technologies that is available to use that can deliver this functionality: we'll see how Bluetooth can help meet this need.

7.1 What Is Bluetooth?

At its essence, wireless communication between two microprocessors is a relatively straightforward concept. It works like this:

1. Take two microprocessors and add a short-range radio transmitter to each of them.

2. These microprocessors can be programmed to send and receive radio signals.

© Philip Meitiner, Pradeeka Seneviratne 2020
P. Meitiner and P. Seneviratne, *Beginning Data Science, IoT, and AI on Single Board Computers*,
https://doi.org/10.1007/978-1-4842-5766-1_7

3. So, we could program one microprocessor to send a
    specific signal over a specific frequency.

4. We could program the other microprocessor to
    listen to that same specific frequency and react
    when a specific signal is received.

5. Our two microprocessors would now be
    communicating wirelessly.

Bluetooth is a set of rules and procedures that govern wireless
communications: it is a standard that people have agreed to follow. It defines
how each of the five components of the process is implemented: How does
the first processor convert data into a specific signal? What frequency is
used? How does the second processor know the message is from the first
one, rather than a malicious third processor?

When humans communicate wirelessly (i.e., talk), we use spoken
language. The words we speak convey meaning, and so too do other
factors, for example, how we emphasize our words, which words we
choose, and how loudly we speak them. We communicate our emotions
as well as our thoughts, and for other people to understand all the depths
and layers of meaning we are communicating, they need to understand the
verbal language we use as well as the "rules" governing the subtleties.
The sound waves that our words make are like the radio signal and
everything else is like the Bluetooth standard.

A deep understanding of the Bluetooth standard is not especially
relevant to us on our data science journey, so we will pick out the
key features we need as the need to use them arises. For now it is
enough to know that Bluetooth is a standard way of managing wireless
communication, and that:

- This standard/list of rules was written down by people and is maintained by people.

- By having an agreed standard, different manufacturers can build "Bluetooth" devices that will be compatible with each other.

- The Bluetooth Special Interest Group (SIG) ensures that the Bluetooth specification is maintained, promoted, protected, and, where necessary, updated. They keep it relevant to the changing technological landscape.

- Where a device follows all the rules laid out in the standard, it is legitimate to refer to it as a **Bluetooth-enabled device**.

7.2 Why Use Bluetooth?

The most compelling reason for us to investigate the suitability of Bluetooth is that the BBC micro:bit has a built-in "Bluetooth Low Energy" (**BLE**) antenna, as is shown in **Figure 7-1**. BLE is a version of Bluetooth that was designed to be very economical in its use of power.

Figure 7-1. *The rear of a micro:bit with BLE antenna circled*

If the onboard BLE is able to meet the needs we identified in **Chapter 6,** then the last piece of our jigsaw is in place and we can add cloud services and IoT to our data science toolkit.

7.3 Using BLE on micro:bit

Our primary objective in using wireless communication is to gather our data and then transmit it to a more suitable location: perhaps to a program like Excel, or to a server 5000 miles away, or maybe even to an artificial intelligence service. Simple!

It will come as a surprise to very few of you to hear that it is not as simple as this: there are some limitations in what can be done with BLE on micro:bit:

There is no option to use BLE with MicroPython.

With MakeCode the most stable implementation of BLE is using a UART cable – so, not wireless.

Despite the limitations, there are still a number of ways in which we can take advantage of BLE in our pursuit of data science, but we need to understand a bit about how BLE handles data first:

- The BLE specification requires a BLE device to have a **profile**, which is information about the device and the data it is able to provide (referred to as a **service**).

- A micro:bit has a profile which defines the data that it will share on request (i.e., the **services** it offers), including data from the accelerometer, magnetometer, onboard temperature sensor, buttons, and a few other bits.

- When another BLE-enabled device **pairs**[1] with the micro:bit, both share their profile, and each can access the data services offered by the other.

- The term **arbitrary data** refers to any data that is not included in the profile. If we add a peripheral to the micro:bit, such as a weather station or CO2 monitor, the data from that peripheral is arbitrary and is not available as a service.

Our scope is broader than just the data that is native to the micro:bit. We might want to measure weather today, CO2 levels tomorrow, and soil acidity the next day. For experiments that just use accelerometer and/or magnetometer data, the micro:bit and BLE are a great tool, but for everything else, we will need another solution.

There are some clever ways in which BLE is used that may be of value to us though, for example, the MakeCode-based **Bluetooth UART** allows us to transfer **arbitrary** data onto a connected smart device; we will look at this in **Section 7.4**. There are also a few other implementations that use a USB cable which are quite stable. But, for any use case where you require the micro:bit to be connected by a USB cable to a computer, the Excel Data Streamer referred to in **Chapter 6** is hard to beat.

---

[1]BLE is a very secure protocol. Before a BLE device will share data with another BLE device, they go through a process of vetting each other, which is referred to as pairing.

7.4 Building a BLE Weather Station with Bluetooth UART

We are going to rebuild the weather station so that it takes advantage of Bluetooth UART: we will feed data from a micro:bit directly to a smart device.

Figure 7-2 shows the block circuit diagram for a BLE-enabled digital weather station instrument.

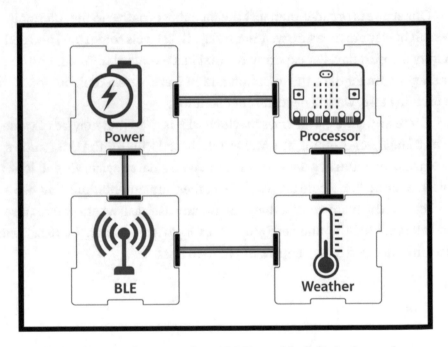

Figure 7-2. *Circuit diagram for a BLE-enabled digital weather station*

Table 7-1 lists the hardware that we will use to build our Bluetooth weather station tool.

Table 7-1. *Hardware requirements for the Bluetooth weather station tool*

What you need	What we use	Qty	Alternatives
A microprocessor and the means to flash code onto it	micro:bit	1	Adafruit Feather 32u4 Bluefruit LE Arduino
Power	2xAAA battery holder with a JST connector	1	Lithium-ion polymer battery – 3.7v
A sensor to read weather data	XinaBox SW01	1	Adafruit BME280 I2C or SPI Temperature Humidity Pressure Sensor
A Bluetooth radio to send weather data to an app	micro:bit built-in Bluetooth radio	1	Adafruit Bluefruit LE Shield
The means to connect it all together	XinaBox IM01 micro:bit bridge and xBus connectors	1 1	Hookup wires

Pick the appropriate tool and assemble the parts as shown in **Figure 7-3**.

Figure 7-3. *Weather station using the micro:bit built-in Bluetooth radio*

7.5 Using the Serial Bluetooth Terminal App

We will use Bluetooth UART to send data to a smartphone/tablet. To do so, our smart device will need to be Bluetooth enabled and we will need to install a compatible app on it. There are plenty of apps to be found on **Google Play** for micro:bit Bluetooth UART; we have tested many of them and found that a few show some success with Bluetooth UART–based data transmission, but we did experience some issues too. We found the best app that provides success most of the time is the **Serial Bluetooth Terminal** app.

The bandwidth of Bluetooth UART is quite low, which means that you can't send a lot of data very quickly. For sending small chunks of data at a time it is quite adequate.

Install the **Serial Bluetooth Terminal** app from **Google Play** for smartphones/tablets running Android OS. Currently, there is no version of this app available for iOS users.

7.6 Coding the BLE Weather Station

The code that we need to write is very similar to our previous weather station code (e.g., **Chapter 3, Section 3-7**): the main difference is that we have to turn on our Bluetooth UART service and output data via that service (rather than outputting the data to a screen). The natural language code has only minor differences.

Table 7-2. *Natural language code for a Bluetooth Low Energy weather station*

Step	Natural Language Code	Notes
1	Import any necessary libraries.	We need a library for the weather sensor and Bluetooth.
2	Start the Bluetooth UART service.	The Bluetooth UART service allows another device such as a smartphone/tablet to exchange any data it wants to with the micro:bit.
3	Repeat the following steps.	
4	Read temperature from the weather sensor.	You could use humidity or pressure if you prefer.
5	Send temperature data through Bluetooth UART.	We output the data by sending it via BLE to the **Serial Bluetooth Terminal** app running on our smart device.

No-code option: You can find a precompiled version of the code used in this section on our **resource website**. Go to http://xib.one/XB and search for **Section 7.6**.

Figure 7-4 shows the full **MakeCode** program for the micro:bit Bluetooth Low Energy weather station.

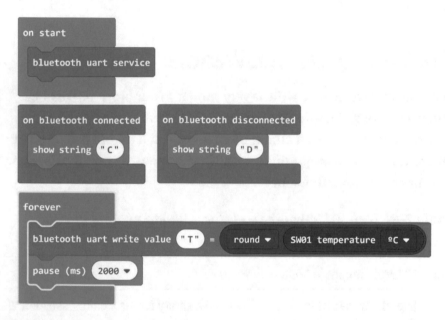

Figure 7-4. *MakeCode blocks to send weather sensor data to the **Serial Bluetooth Terminal** app running on a smartphone/tablet*

Note   The code is written to send temperature only. By modifying it you can add humidity and pressure data too. But the more data you send at once, the greater the chance that you will encounter difficulties due to low bandwidth. This solution does not scale well if we want to send several data points at the same time.

There is one more thing to do before downloading the code to flash onto the micro:bit:

- Go to **Project Settings** (click the **cog-wheel** at the top-right corner of the page).

- Choose **No Pairing Required: Anyone can connect via Bluetooth** option (**Figure 7-5**).

- Click **Save** to save the new settings and go back to the editor.

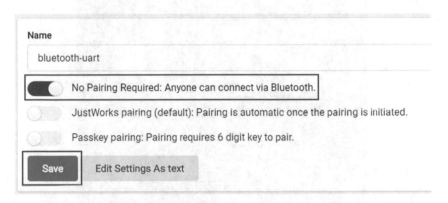

Figure 7-5. *Configuration settings for the Bluetooth UART*

Now compile your program and flash it onto your micro:bit. Reset your micro:bit and keep it powered up.

Start the **Serial Bluetooth Terminal** app installed on your smartphone/tablet, and from the menu (top-left corner) select **Devices ➤ BLUETOOTH LE**. Then select the name of your micro:bit from the list. The app will connect to your micro:bit. At the same time, the letter "C" will display on the micro:bit 5X5 LED matrix. After that, the temperature data will display on the app's terminal (**Figure 7-6**).

Note   Sometimes your app might not connect to the micro:bit at the first attempt. Try a few more times and if that doesn't solve the problem, restart the app/micro:bit. If that still doesn't work after a few times then try Wi-Fi, which we will look at in **Chapter 9**.

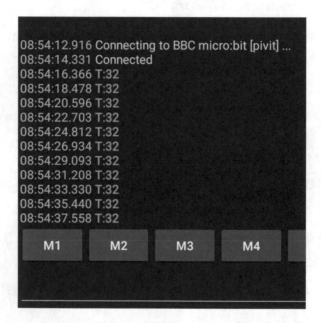

Figure 7-6. *Sensor data is displaying on the app's terminal*

We have succeeded in extracting data wirelessly from our micro:bit. The tools that are available in the application you are using to view this data are now available.

Closing the app will disconnect the BLE connection between your smartphone/tablet and the micro:bit.

7.7 Other Options for BLE on micro:bit

Support for BLE is not available in MicroPython and is limited in MakeCode, but there are many other ways to code a micro:bit: it is possible to develop applications in platforms such as ArduinoIDE or mBed that open up what can be achieved. Our website includes an application we have put together that uses ArduinoIDE to build a BLE-enabled weather station for micro:bit which can connect to the IoT.

This example begins to show the real potential of BLE on micro:bit, but it is complex and long, not suitable for learners or beginners and way more complicated than other potential solutions, which we will begin to look at in later chapters.

7.8 Summary

The version of Bluetooth that is available on micro:bit (**BLE**) provides some tools that have the potential to be quite useful to us in our data science endeavors. If all we need is the data that is native to a micro:bit, or if limited data is acceptable, or if a wired solution is adequate, then BLE has a lot to offer. But these limitations feel restrictive and BLE does not give us free and easy access to the Internet of Things or the cloud.

At the beginning of this chapter, we set out to identify a way of extracting data wirelessly from the micro:bit; while BLE has some very interesting and useful applications, it also has limitations.

We are going to add BLE to our toolkit, but we will continue our search for a wireless solution. BLE has a lot to offer and is a very promising technology, but as long as we use the micro:bit as the core of our data gathering tool, the limitations will restrict our capabilities.

CHAPTER 8

Investigating the micro:bit Radio

In **Chapter 7** we saw that the BLE offering on micro:bit is comprised of two completely different components:

- A physical, onboard radio transmitter/receiver (antenna)

- The BLE standards that govern what is transmitted, how it is transmitted and how messages received are handled

BLE acts as a manager: it governs how the antenna is used but is completely separate from the antenna. It is possible to bypass BLE and access the radio directly, to manage the antenna ourselves. This chapter will look at how we can use the micro:bit radio to bring value to our data science toolkit.

8.1 Standards Are Important

One of the things that BLE does well is it allows the micro:bit to communicate with other (BLE-enabled) devices. It can pair with mobile phones, tablets, and laptops, but not with other micro:bits.

P. Meitiner and P. Seneviratne, *Beginning Data Science, IoT, and AI on Single Board Computers*, https://doi.org/10.1007/978-1-4842-5766-1_8

Without the BLE standard to manage radio communication we will face the same problem we might encounter listening to someone speaking in a language we are not familiar with: we hear the sounds they are making but we cannot extract meaning from them. Two radios can transmit and receive signals till the cows come home: unless there is a common language that both the transmitter and the receiver have agreed to use, they will not be able to make sense of each other.

Some kind of communication standard is necessary: if we drop BLE we will have to replace it with something else. Both MakeCode and MicroPython provide an alternative, much simpler, way of using the onboard radio.

8.2 Using Radio for Input/Output

We have already seen how to write data to the micro:bit's memory, how to print data to a screen and how to transmit data over a BLE connection. In all these cases, what we are doing is very similar: we are outputting data. Radio is just another place that we can output data to: instead of telling the microprocessor to send data to a screen or file, we tell it to transmit it from the antenna.

Both MicroPython and MakeCode provide tools to use the onboard antenna as a data communication tool. The standards that they apply are different; the main consequence of which is that a micro:bit running code written in MicroPython cannot communicate by radio with a micro:bit programmed in MakeCode.

Both MakeCode and MicroPython provide the basic functionality needed to use the antenna: they allow data to be converted into radio signals, transmitted wirelessly and then, when received, converted back into data. We know that if we convert (for example) the number "4" or the word "hello" into a radio signal which is transmitted, then a micro:bit at the other end receiving this signal will be able to interpret the signal to mean "4" or "hello". But there is still work for us to do in the code, as we will see.

A constraint with the onboard radio is that it only enables micro:bits to communicate with other micro:bits. We can use it build a closed network of micro:bits that can communicate among themselves. How can we use this meaningfully in our data science endeavors?

8.3 Using Radio to Build a Network

In **Chapter** 1 we saw that thermometers record ambient temperature, which is the temperature of a very small volume of space in the vicinity of the sensor.

To measure the temperature of a room/large area, such that we can be confident in our result, it helps to sample several different locations and derive an answer based on multiple data points. The micro:bit radio is the perfect tool for this.

What we will do is build a small network of micro:bits; we use four, two will do, and the exercise will scale up to many more. Our network will behave as described:

- We are going get four micro:bits that communicate with each other over radio.

- One of the micro:bits on the network will be different from the others: we will call this one our **server** or **collector** and it will have the job of listening out for radio signals from other micro:bits in the network.

- The other three micro:bits are **nodes**. They are identical, and their job is to measure temperature and transmit the result.

- The server will listen for temperature data from the micro:bits in the network. When it has received data from all of them it aggregates it and shows the average.

Figure 8-1 depicts a simple radio-based network of micro:bits, with three nodes and one server.

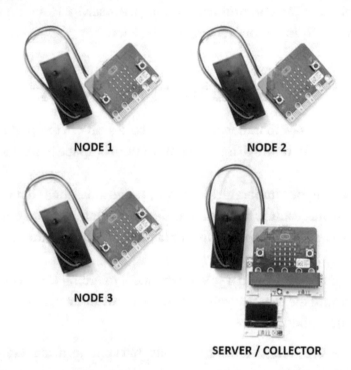

NODE 1

NODE 2

NODE 3

SERVER / COLLECTOR

Figure 8-1. *Our network consists of four separate instruments*

8.4 Choosing MakeCode or MicroPython

There are some subtle differences between how MicroPython and MakeCode handle radio communication. Most obvious of these is with groups/channels:

- In MakeCode there are 256 groups ranging from 0 to 255. To use the radio feature on a micro:bit, you have to assign it to a group.

- In MicroPython the are 84 (some sources claim 100) channels, numbered 0–83, that you can use to transmit/ receive.

For the remainder of this chapter we are going to use MakeCode: our objective is to understand what value radio on the micro:bit can add to our data science experimentation, and MakeCode is slightly simpler to use. In addition, avoiding having to consider subtle but arbitrary differences in how MakeCode and MicroPython implement radio will ensure we stay focused on the core message.

8.5 MakeCode Radio Groups

When we send data over radio, let's say the number "4", the MakeCode standard pads it with other data, such as the **group ID**. So, when you tell MakeCode to send "4", what is actually transmitted might look more like "32_4" (which is simplified, but makes the point). All the data is sent together and is referred to as a **packet**.

Micro:bit broadcasts its **group ID** inside each data **packet**. In addition, a micro:bit will ONLY process messages that include the same group ID. **Figure 8-2** shows six micro:bits deployed as two groups.

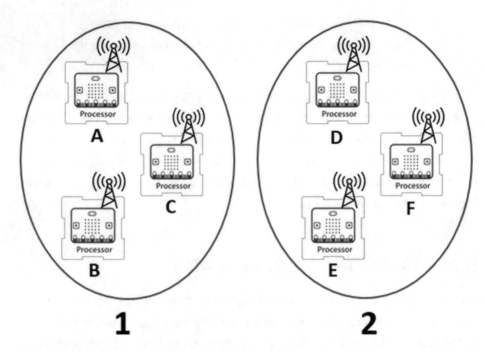

Figure 8-2. *Six micro:bits deployed as two groups*

In group 1 micro:bits A, B, and C all transmit the same group ID when they send packets, and they only process packets they receive that include that group ID. They can communicate with each other, but they cannot communicate with micro:bits D, E, and F in group 2. The micro:bits in group 2 ignore any messages coming from group 1 and vice versa.

Micro:bit radio doesn't perform one-way or two-way communication. Instead it broadcasts data just like a radio station broadcasts music and voice. If any micro:bit wants to receive the data broadcasted by another micro:bit, they just need to be in the same group.

8.6 Nodes and a Collector

To build our networked thermometer we will design a simple radio network that consists of a few **nodes** and a **collector**:

- A node collects data and transmits it to other micro:bits in the same group.

- The collector listens for data from nodes and acts on that data in some predetermined way.

The example we will use includes three nodes and one collector. You can adapt the network size by adding or removing nodes; if so you will need to modify the code. A micro:bit network of up to ten nodes should be relatively stable.

Figure 8-3 shows the radio network we will build:

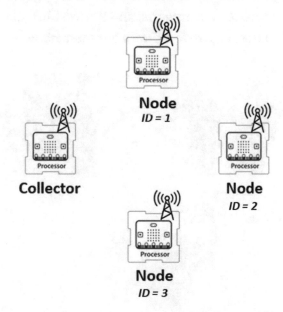

Figure 8-3. *Our simple radio network with three nodes and a collector*

Each **node** has a unique ID, which we will define in the code. They each measure the **ambient temperature** (using the built-in micro:bit thermometer) and then broadcast the temperature and their **Node ID**. A time delay, 5 seconds, will be implemented in between.

The **collector** will monitor radio transmissions. When it receives a message with the right **Node ID** it will extract both the **temperature** and the **Node ID** from the packet. It will wait until all the nodes in the network have reported their temperature; then it will work out the mean temperature, which it will display.

8.7 Building the Nodes

We are going to **build three nodes**. The hardware required for each node is very simple: just a micro:bit and a power supply. We will use the onboard temperature sensor, antenna, and the 5x5 LED matrix to display a "**message sent**" status. **Figure 8-4** shows our three nodes.

NODE 1   NODE 2

NODE 3

Figure 8-4. *Three micro:bit temperature sensor nodes*

The code we need to write is illustrated in natural language in **Figure 8-5**.

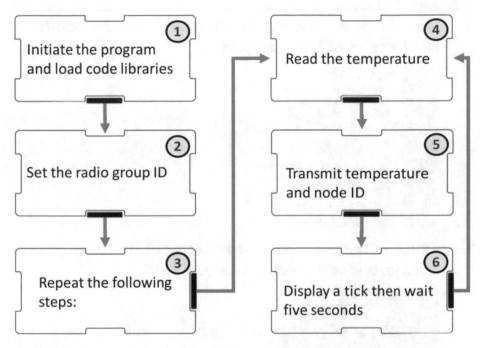

Figure 8-5. *Natural language code for our sensor nodes*

No-code option: You can find a precompiled version of the code used in this section on our **resource website**. Go to http://xib.one/XB and search for **Section 8.7**.

Table 8-1 shows how to convert the natural language code earlier into **MakeCode** blocks that can be compiled and loaded into your **nodes**.

Table 8-1.   *Developing code for sensor nodes with MakeCode blocks*

Step	Description
1	Make sure your MakeCode project has the **Radio** extension. If not, add it to the project using the **Extensions** option.

| 2 | Add the **radio set group** block to the **on start** block. Use the default **group ID** unless you need a different one (valid range: 0–255). |

Note	Use the same group ID for all the nodes.

| 3 | Repeat the following. |

(continued)

Table 8-1. (*continued*)

Step	Description

4   Add the **radio send value** block to the **forever** block.

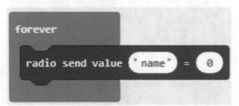

This will send data as a "name-value pair": we will send our **Node ID** as the name and temperature as the value.

5   Type the **Node ID** in the **name** box. Use *different* **Node IDs** for other nodes.

Then add the **temperature** block onto the **value** box:

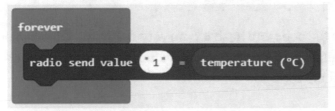

6   Add the following blocks after the **radio send value** block:

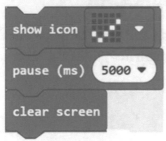

The **show icon** block is used to display a **tick** on the micro:bit 5x5 LED matrix after a packet sent.

The **pause** block is used to send data every 5 seconds.

Figure 8-6 shows the **MakeCode** blocks for the micro:bit sensor
node 1.

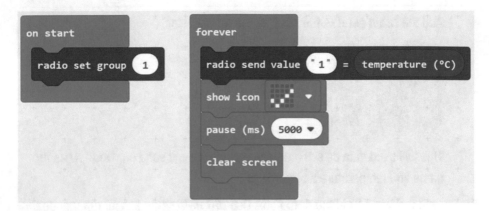

Figure 8-6. *MakeCode blocks for sensor node 1. It is in radio group 1
and its Node ID is 1*

Now compile the code and flash it onto your micro:bit. Label it Node 1;
then change the code (just the **radio send value** block) for your other
nodes and flash them too.

8.8 Building the Server/Collector

Our **server/collector** will also use a micro:bit and power supply, but we
will add an OLED display to view the data (**Figure 8-7**).

Figure 8-7. *The server/collector*

The way that the code needs to work is outlined in natural language in **Figure 8-8**.

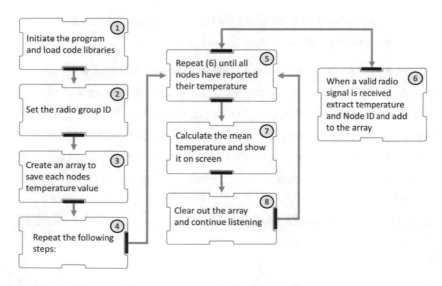

Figure 8-8. *Natural language code for the collector*

No-code option: Our **resource website** has versions of the server/ collector code for 1, 2, 3, and 4 nodes. Go to `http://xib.one/XB` and search for **Section 8.10**.

While the natural language code is relatively simple, converting it into MakeCode blocks (or MicroPython) will be daunting for an inexperienced programmer. We are effectively building a server, a very simple one, but nonetheless it is a nontrivial programming task.

The full MakeCode block program, several pages of it, is shown in **Figure 8-9**. If you are interested in looking at how each step of the natural language code translates into blocks, please check out the supporting website.

If you are less interested in the code and more interested in the data science applications that the instruments can support, then ask yourself the following questions:

1.   Could you adapt the code so that it works for other measures, for example, humidity or C02 levels?

2.   Could you adapt the code to add in more nodes?

3.   Could you describe what you need to a programmer so that they could adapt the code?

If you answered yes to (3), then it really doesn't matter if you can program or not. Being a strong programmer is a great skill for a data scientist to have, but you can be a great data scientist without it. In later chapters we will connect to Wi-Fi, build an IoT application and communicate with an artificial intelligence. In none of these instances will the code we use be anywhere near as complex as the following code. Noncoders: please persevere!

Figure 8-9 shows the **MakeCode** blocks for the micro:bit collector.

Section 1:

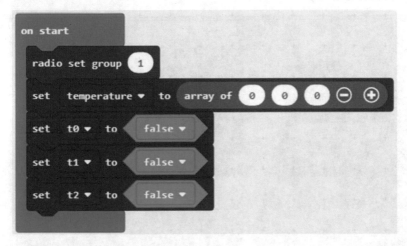

Section 2:

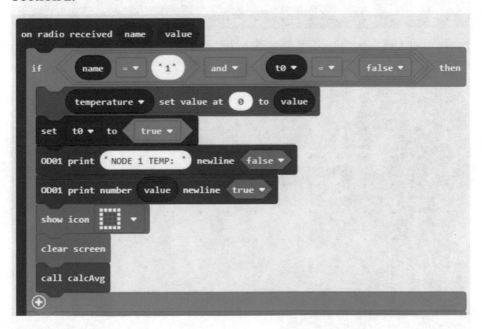

Figure 8-9. *MakeCode blocks for the micro:bit collector*

Section 2:   (continued)

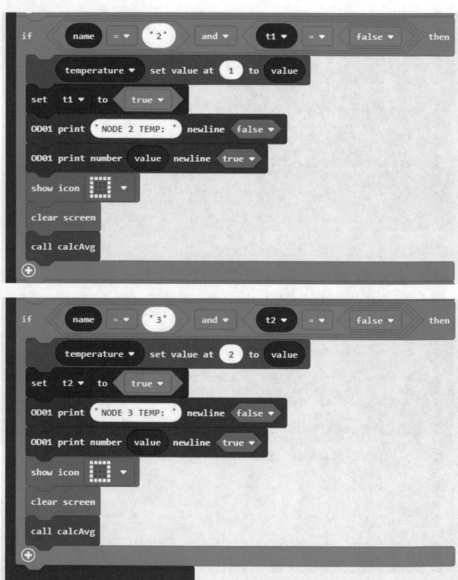

Figure 8-9. *(continued)*

Section 3:

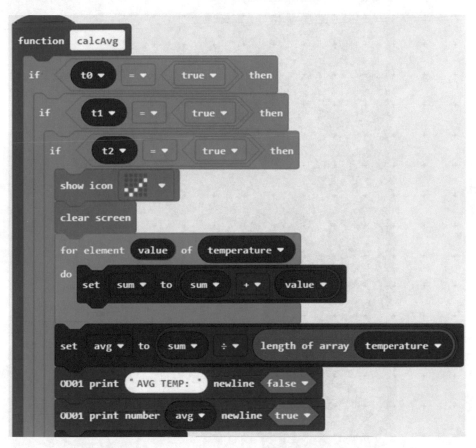

Figure 8-9. *(continued)*

Section 3:   (continued)

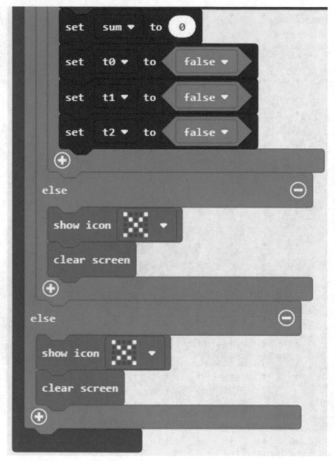

Figure 8-9. (continued)

Flash the code onto the collector and then power it up. Make sure the nodes are powered up too.

The collector will listen to the group 1 channel and, when it receives a message from one of the nodes it is programmed to listen out for, it will extract the temperature data from that message and display it on screen. When data from all the nodes has been received the collector will display the average temperature on the OLED screen (**Figure 8-10**).

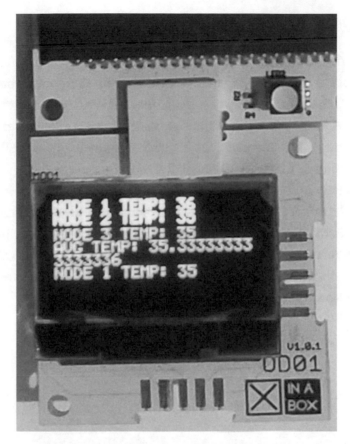

Figure 8-10. *The OLED screen displays temperature from each sensor node and the calculated average temperature*

Test your network by placing the nodes in remote locations: how far away from the collector can they be and how important is "line of sight" to the range? The node code could be adapted to send other types of data, and we have seen in earlier chapters how to add sensors to a micro:bit. What sensors could you add to the network to provide useful data?

8.9 Summary

The radio functionality can be used to create closed networks of micro:bits that are able to communicate with each other. The example we built earlier could be extended: up to ten micro:bits should work together on a network. With several nodes of multiple sensors reporting data to a server, you could monitor and control an office, classroom, exotic pet habitat, nuclear reactor or any area served by the range of the radio.

But as long as these networks are closed we will not be able to harness the potential of IoT and our scope will be limited by the capabilities of the micro:bit. Radio provides functionality that can be harnessed in our data science endeavors, but until we can connect to the cloud and consume the services available there our toolkit is incomplete. In **Chapter** 9 we will add Wi-Fi to micro:bit and finally open a window into IoT.

CHAPTER 9

Using Wi-Fi to Connect to the Internet

In **Chapter 6** we saw that being able to hook up our experiments to the Internet has the potential to greatly enhance our data science toolkit. In **Chapter 7** and **Chapter 8** we looked to see if the functionality on board the micro:bit could connect us to the cloud, to give us access to the services available there. Although both BLE and the micro:bit radio provide some really useful wireless functionality, we are still no closer to connecting properly to the IoT than we were several chapters ago. It is time to look beyond the native functionality of the micro:bit.

Connecting to the IoT is relatively simple these days and most commonly done using Wi-Fi.[1] In this chapter we will add Wi-Fi to our micro:bit weather station and connect it to the cloud.

---

[1]Most people agree that the acronym **Wi-Fi** originates from the phrase "Wireless Fidelity." In fact Wi-Fi is a trademarked term for **IEEE 802.11x**, which is a standard for wireless communication (as, of course, is Bluetooth). It differs from Bluetooth in the purposes for which it is best suited. Bluetooth is used over a shorter range to connect two devices together securely (e.g., to connect headphones to a mobile phone). Wi-Fi has a higher range and speed, consumes less power, and is designed to provide the communication network for the Internet.

For our purposes we can understand Wi-Fi as the means by which a smart device can share data wirelessly with the Internet.

© Philip Meitiner, Pradeeka Seneviratne 2020
P. Meitiner and P. Seneviratne, *Beginning Data Science, IoT, and AI on Single Board Computers*, https://doi.org/10.1007/978-1-4842-5766-1_9

9.1 Defining Our IoT Weather Station

Just adding Wi-Fi to our micro:bit weather station is all well and good, but what does this actually mean: what is it that we are going to build? We need a much clearer idea of how we want the system to work:

1. Our micro:bit weather station is not going to change much: we will record temperature, humidity, and pressure data. We will just output that data over Wi-Fi this time.

2. We are going to connect the micro:bit weather station to an IoT platform.

3. We will send the weather data to the IoT platform.

4. When the data is in the platform we will have access to a number of tools/services. We will build a chart that shows the data in real time and compares it to historical data.

As we saw in **Chapter 6**, once the data is in our IoT platform, we will have access to a range of tools that we can use in our data science undertakings. In **Section 9.4** we will set up our IoT platform, but first we'll sort out the hardware that we need.

9.2 Building Our Wi-Fi Weather Station

In addition to the hardware we used in **Chapter 8,** we need to introduce a module that provides Wi-Fi connectivity. **Figure 9-1** shows the block diagram for a Wi-Fi-enabled digital weather station instrument.

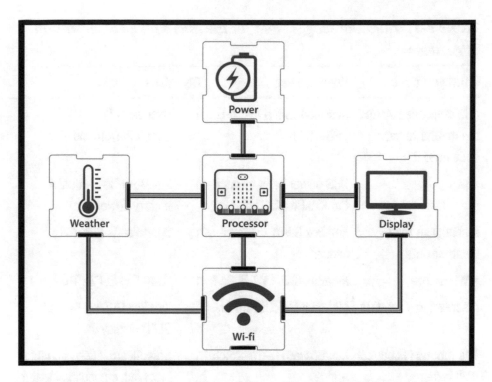

Figure 9-1. *Components required for a Wi-Fi-enabled weather station tool*

Table 9-1 lists the specific hardware we used to build our micro:bit weather station edge device.

Table 9-1. *Hardware suggestions for the micro:bit weather station edge device*

What you need	What we use	Qty	Alternatives
A microprocessor and the means to flash code onto it	micro:bit with a micro-B USB cable	1	Raspberry Pi Circuit Playground
Power	USB power bank through the XinaBox IM01	1	XinaBox PB01 – dual AA battery power pack
A sensor to read weather data	XinaBox SW01 weather sensor	1	SparkFun Weatherbit
A Wi-Fi core	XinaBox CW01 Wi-Fi Core	1	SparkFun ESP32 Thing
A screen to view data	Micro:bit 5x5 LED matrix	1	XinaBox OD01 – 64x128 OLED display
The means to connect it all together	XinaBox IM01 – micro:bit bridge	1	Breadboard, edge connector breakout, crocodile/alligator leads, and hookup wires
	xBus connectors	2	

Figure 9-2 shows what the micro:bit weather station edge device looks like when assembled.

Figure 9-2. *micro:bit weather station with Wi-Fi*

9.3 Updating Firmware

Firmware is a computer program on a microprocessor that serves as its operating system. Code that we write (in MakeCode/MicroPython) and flash onto our micro:bits is a set of instructions that the firmware interprets: our programs tell the firmware what to do.

The BBC micro:bit was first released almost 5 years ago and in that time it hasn't really changed. Earlier versions of the micro:bit firmware do not support Wi-Fi: you may need to update yours, not just for this chapter but for the example in **Chapter 11** too.

It is good practice to ensure that your firmware is always up to date, so if you haven't updated it recently we recommend that you do so before continuing. It is very easy: little more than flashing a file onto the micro:bit, and will ensure that all the latest releases and advanced functionality work properly on your micro:bit. You can find full instructions on our resource website, or on the Micro:bit Foundation's website.

Although we only use it for its Wi-Fi capabilities, the CW01 from XinaBox is also a microprocessor; it too has firmware loaded onto it. To use the CW01 with micro:bit, it is necessary to ensure it is running the correct firmware. Most readers will NOT need to update the firmware though; it all depends on where you got the CW01 from:

- If the CW01 was part of the XinaBox XK05 kit then it does NOT need to be updated.

- If you bought the CW01 by itself, or it came with a different kit (e.g., the XK01), you will need to update it.

Full instructions for updating the CW01 firmware are available on our resource website.

Before proceeding please ensure that both the micro:bit and the CW01 are running suitable firmware.

9.4 Choosing an IoT Platform

To build an IoT weather station, we need to choose an IoT platform to use. There are a range of options, some more simple than others.

The MakeCode extension for the CW01 Wi-Fi module from XinaBox has blocks that are tailored to connect easily to Ubidots, ATT, and Azure.

It also has "generic" MQTT[2] blocks, which allow you to connect to any IoT platform that follows the MQTT standard.

We will use the **IBM Cloud** as our exemplar, for the following reasons:

- We had to choose one, and IBM have always been at the forefront of IoT.

- Showing how to use the MQTT blocks in MakeCode will better equip you to connect to any IoT platform. The tailored blocks are easier to use, but can only be used with the IoT platform they are tailored to.

- You will have access to a broad range of IBM Cloud services (including the IBM Watson AI services).

- They offer a free 28-day service so you can test it without needing to pay.

To sign up for an IBM Cloud, you need to have an **IBMid**. This allows you to log in to all IBM products and services. If you don't have one already, the following steps explain how to sign up using your email address:

Warning   We found that outlook email addresses can't be used to create IBM Cloud accounts. Gmail works.

- Go to the IBM Cloud login page (`https://cloud.ibm.com/login`), and click **Create an IBM Cloud account** (**Figure 9-3**).

---

[2]MQTT (Message Queuing Telemetry Transport) is a wireless communication standard. It is not a competitor to Wi-Fi (or Bluetooth): it is a standard that applies to messages sent using Wi-Fi. It is enough for our needs to know that most IoT platforms will be MQTT compliant. If you know how to connect to one MQTT IoT platform, then you should be able to connect to others.

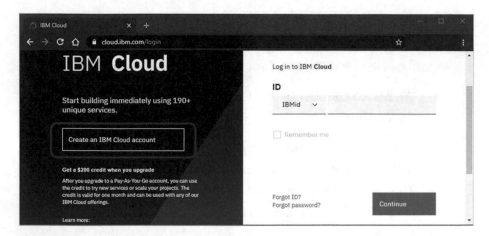

Figure 9-3.   *IBM Cloud login page*

- Enter your **email address**.

- Complete the remaining fields and then click **Create
  Account**.

- The next page will show you if your account has been
  created successfully (**Figure 9-4**).

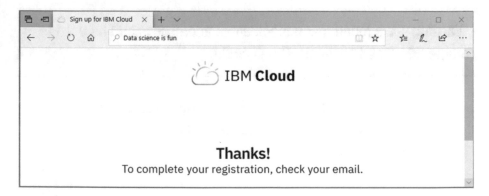

Figure 9-4.   *Account creation success message*

- Check your email, and then confirm your account by clicking **Confirm account** in the confirmation email you are sent.

- You will be taken to the login page. Click **Log in** to proceed.

- You will be redirected to the **About your IBMid Account Privacy** page. Ensure you are happy with the privacy policy before scrolling down the page to find the **Proceed** button.

- You will be automatically logged in to the **IBM Cloud Dashboard** (**Figure 9-5**).

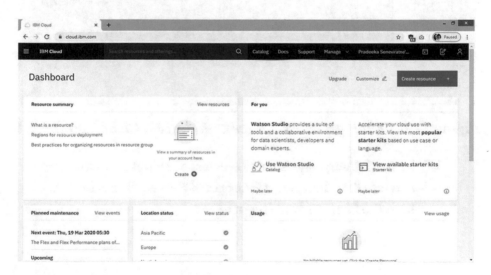

Figure 9-5. *IBM Cloud Dashboard*

The IBM Cloud Dashboard is the hub from which you can access all the IBM products and services.

9.5 Setting Up the IoT Platform

The service that we will connect our micro:bit weather station to is the aptly named **IBM Internet of Things Platform**, which is accessed from the IBM Cloud Dashboard, as described here:

- In the IBM Cloud Dashboard, click **Create resource** (**Figure 9-6**).

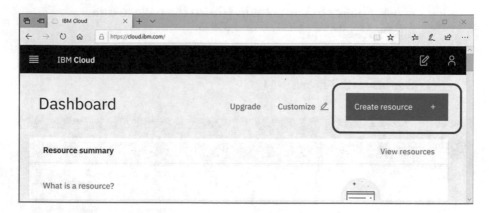

Figure 9-6. *Creating a new resource with the IBM Cloud Dashboard*

- In the **Catalog** page, select **Internet of Things** from the Services list. Then select **Internet of Things Platform** from the filtered result (**Figure 9-7**).

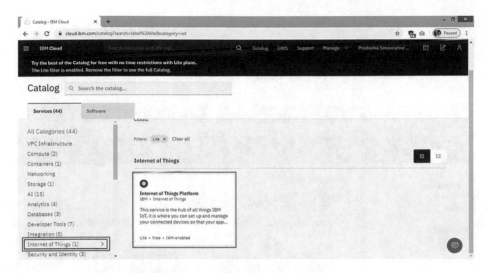

Figure 9-7. *Selecting Internet of Things Platform service*

- Select the **Lite Plan**.

- Scroll down the page and rename the service name
  (e.g., **Weather Service**) (**Figure 9-8**).

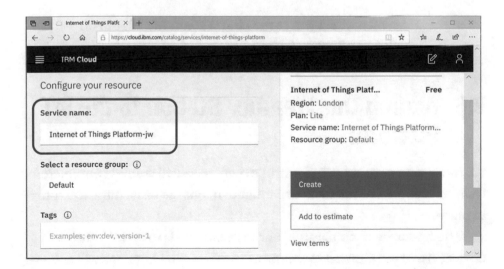

Figure 9-8. *Renaming the default service name*

- Click **Create**. After a few seconds, the service will be created.

- Click **Launch** (**Figure 9-9**).

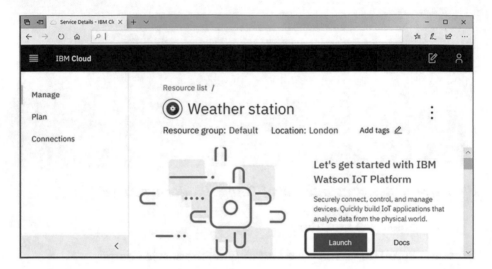

Figure 9-9. *Launch page for our weather service*

- This will redirect you to the **IBM Watson IoT Platform**, which we will set up in the next section.

9.6 Adding Our Weather Station to the IoT Platform

We have now set up an IoT platform to which we will connect our micro:bit weather station. We still need to configure it, but the basic infrastructure is in place.

The first stage in configuring our IoT platform is to identify the device(s) that are allowed to connect to it. The following steps will achieve this objective:

- Click **Add Device** at the top right of the page
  (**Figure 9-10**).

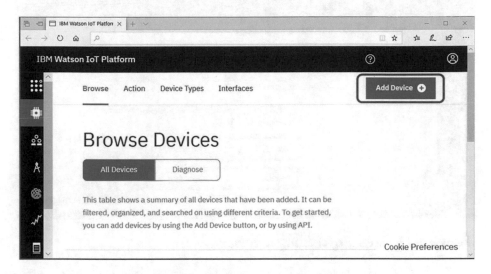

Figure 9-10. *Adding a new device*

- In the **Add Device** window, enter a name and unique
  ID for the device and then click **Next** (**Figure 9-11**).
  We used the details listed:

  - **Device Type**: *XinaBox*

  - **Device ID**: *xb123456*

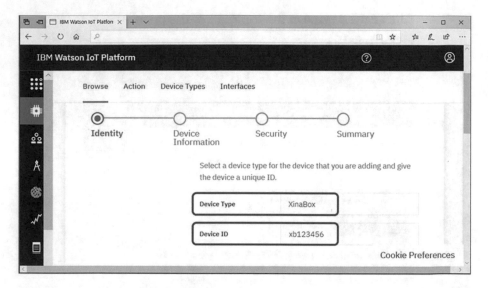

Figure 9-11. *Step 1 of adding a device*

- In the **Device Information** tab, leave all the device information blank and click **Next**.

- In the **Security** tab, leave **Authentication Token** blank (to let the Authentication Token be auto-generated). Click **Next**.

- In the **Summary** tab, click **Finish**.

- The next page shows the **Device Credentials** (**Figure 9-12**).

Warning   It was not clear how to retrieve the Authentication Token once you go away from this page. Remember to take a screenshot of that page or write down the device credentials on a paper. You will need them when you build the code.

Figure 9-12. *Device Credentials for the device we have just added*

- Click **Back** at the top left of the page to see all devices that have been added. Your device will show in the device list.

- Click **Security** in the left navigation (**Figure 9-13**).

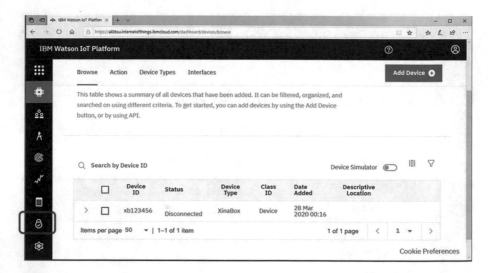

Figure 9-13. *The Security tab is available in the left-hand-side menu*

- In the **Policies** page, click **edit** to edit the **Connection Security (Figure 9-14)**.

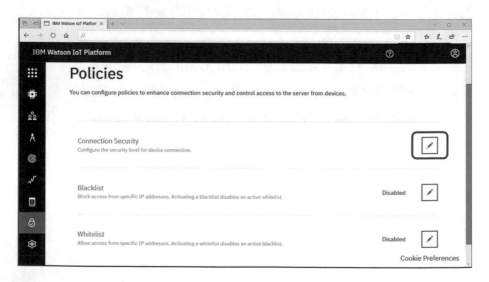

Figure 9-14. *The Policies page*

- Choose *TLS Optional* from the *Security Level* drop-
  down list (**Figure 9-15**). Then click *Save* at the top right.

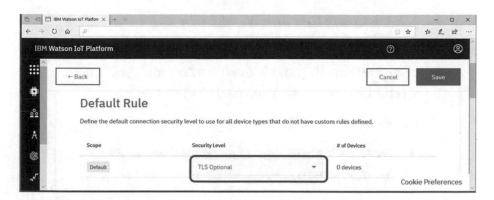

Figure 9-15. *The security level chosen for the default rule applies to all your devices*

In **Section 9.5** we set up the shell of our "IoT application" and in this section we defined key parameters relating to the device we will connect to it. What remains is to tell our IoT application what to do with data that we will send to it from that device.

9.7 Visualizing Data in the IoT Platform

In this section we will tell our IoT platform what to do with the data and how to output/display it. We will build a visualization: a line chart.

IBM Watson allows us to set up virtual "pin-boards" to which we can add all sorts of different content. Later, when everything is running smoothly, we will be able to view these pin-boards (referred to as **boards**) from a browser.

The content that we add to a board is called a **card**. Cards are predefined items (e.g., a line chart) that are used to show data from or about the device(s) defined in our IoT platform. We can add multiple cards to a board. In this section we will create a new **Board** in the Watson Internet of Things Dashboard and then add a **Card** to it.

Add a new board using the following steps:

- Click **Boards** in the left navigation.

- Click **+ Create New Board**.

- In the **Create a new board** window, in the
  Information tab, provide the following configuration
  details (**Figure 9-16**). Then click the **Next** button.

  - **Board name**: *Weather*

  - **Description**: *Displays sensor data from various
    weather sensors.*

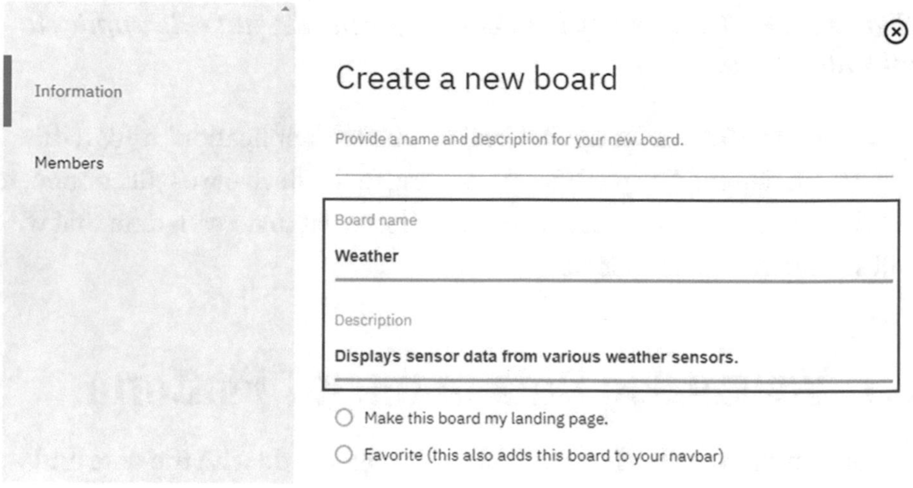

Figure 9-16. *Creating a new dashboard: the Information tab*

- In the **Members** tab don't provide any information. Just
  click **Submit**.

- The **board** will be created and the **Your boards** page
  will load up (**Figure 9-17**).

Figure 9-17. *The newly created board showing under Your boards*

We now have an empty pin-board to which we can add cards; we will add a line chart card to show the weather data as it is received. This line chart will show temperature and relative humidity data (not pressure – this messes up the chart because the scale used for pressure is so different). You will see that there are a range of different cards that you can add to the board.

- Click the **WEATHER** board.

- Click + **Add New Card**.

- In the **Create card** window, click the **Line chart** (**Figure 9-18**).

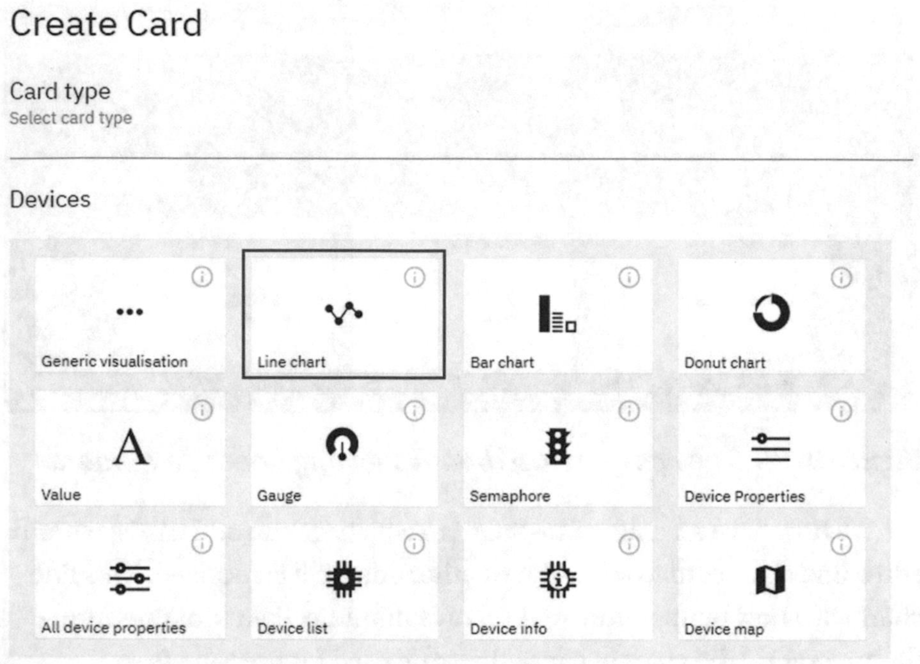

Create Card

Card type
Select card type

Devices

Figure 9-18. *Choosing the line chart data visualization option*

- In the **Create Line chart Card** window, in the **Card source data** tab, select the **device** you created earlier and click **Next** (**Figure 9-19**).

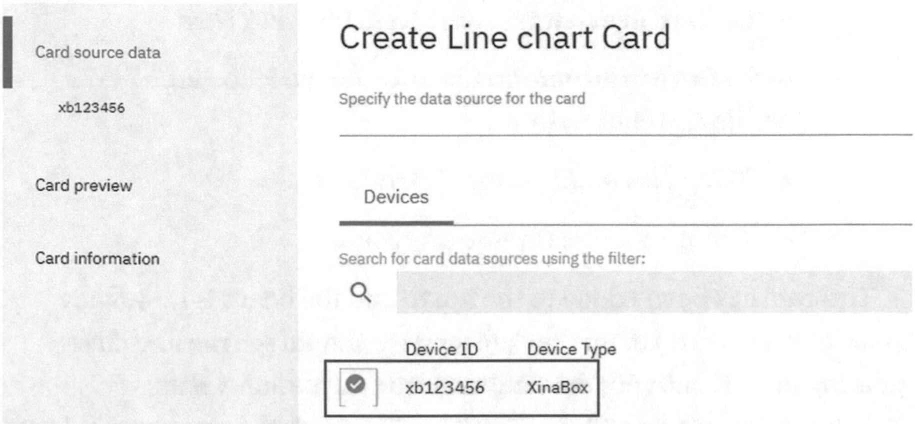

Figure 9-19. *Choosing the device*

- Click to select the **xb123456** device (rem – this is the
  Device ID we specified in **Section 9-6**) and then click **Next**.

In this step we have linked the micro:bit edge device to the line chart.
We now need to tell the line chart which data to use and how to handle
it. We will add two data sets (temperature and humidity); we need to add
these **New data sets** with the details in **Table 9-2**.

Table 9-2. *Parameters to use to set up the line chart card*

Name of data point you need to enter	Value to enter for temperature	Value to enter for humidity
Event	status1	status2
Property	Temperature	Humidity
Name	Temperature	Humidity
Type	Number	Number
Unit	C	%
Min	-40	0
Max	85	100

- In the **Card preview** tab, click **XL**. Then click **Next**.

- In the **Card information** tab, provide the following details and click **Submit**.

  - **Title**: *Live and Historical Weather Data*

  - **Color scheme**: Choose any color

The card has been added to the board and the board is now ready to use: as soon as we set up the data feed we should see the line chart updating in real time with the temperature and humidity data.

Other cards can be added to the board in much the same way. Why not add a card to visualize the pressure data too.

9.8 Coding Our Wi-Fi Weather Station

In this section we will write the code required to make the micro:bit behave like a digital weather station; we set up the IoT platform first as there are details from it that we need to include in the code. **Figure 9-20** outlines the program flow in natural language.

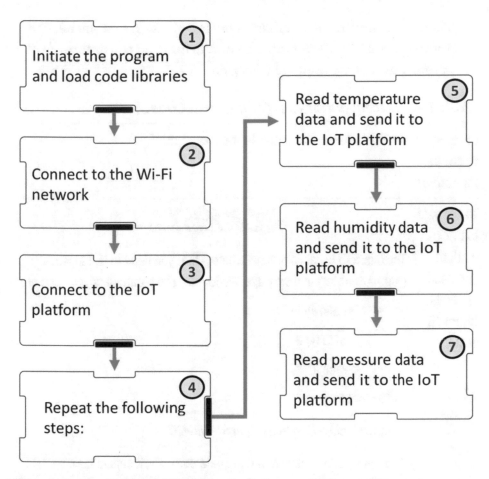

Figure 9-20. *Natural language code for our IoT weather station*

Figure 9-20 includes two steps that we haven't encountered before:

> **Step 2**: Connect to the Wi-Fi network. To connect
> to a Wi-Fi network you will need to know its name
> (**SSID**) and **password**. Have these handy before you
> start writing the code.

> **Step 3**: Connect to the IoT platform. This is
> explained in **Table 9-3**.

There are a number of details from the IoT platform that you need to enter into the code. **Table 9-3** explains how to find and construct each of the parameters that are used in MakeCode.

Table 9-3. *Setting parameters for the MakeCode blocks*

Parameter to set in MakeCode	Where to find/how to create the parameter
To connect to the IoT platform, you need to set the **Client ID** value.	`CW01 set MQTT client ID` The Client ID consists of 3 parameters that you need to join together ("**concatenate**") in a very specific format. The parameters you need are • Organization ID • Device type • Device ID The format is ***d:Organization-ID:Device-Type:Device-ID*** When you have concatenated the data correctly, it should look something like this: **d:oprah53:XinaBox:xb123456**

(*continued*)

Table 9-3. (*continued*)

Parameter to set in MakeCode	Where to find/how to create the parameter
To connect to the IoT platform, you need to set 3 values in the **Connect to the MQTT broker** block.	 You need to enter 3 parameters into the **Connect to the MQTT broker** block for this:

1. The **broker URL** (or "connection address")

*Add the **organization ID** to the front of the string ".messaging. internetofthings.ibmcloud.com"*

*A correct **broker URL** looks like this:*

opra53. messaging.internetofthings.ibmcloud.com

2. The **user name**

The fixed string "use-token-auth" is entered here.

3. The **password**

*The password is the **Authentication Token** specified in the **Device Credentials** section.*

(*continued*)

Table 9-3. (*continued*)

Parameter to set in MakeCode	Where to find/how to create the parameter
To pass data to the IoT platform, you need to send a **payload** to a specific **topic**.	 What we send to the IoT platform is referred to as the **payload** and we have to specify where we want to send it to: the **topic**. 1. The **payload** We have to concatenate 3 bits to build the payload. Choose a Join block and add the following elements: • {" *[variable name]*": " • The value that you want to send • "} So, if you are sending temperature data, the join block will look something like this:

![payload join "{"temperature":"" round ▾ SW01 temperature ℃ ▾ ""}" ⊖ ⊕]

(continued)

Table 9-3. (*continued*)

Parameter to set in MakeCode	Where to find/how to create the parameter

2. The **topic**

The topic is a string which tells the IoT platform which card to pass the data to, and which data point it is. The format for the topic is ***iot-2/evt/<Event>/fmt/json***.

A valid topic will look something like this:

iot-2/evt/status1/fmt/json

The **<Event>** is the Event name you entered when setting up the card, in **Edit Line chart Card > connect data set:**

Edit Line chart Card

Connect data set

≡   temperature

Event

status1

Table 9-4 shows how to convert the code from **Figure 9-20** into MakeCode blocks using the parameters outlined in **Table 9-3**.

Table 9-4. *Developing code with MakeCode blocks*

Step	Description
1	Start a new project. Add the XinaBox **SW01** and **CW01** extensions.
2	Add the **CW01 connect to WiFi** block to the **on start** block.

This will connect your CW01 to a Wi-Fi network.

3	**Connect to the IoT platform/set Client ID:**

- Add a **CW01 set MQTT client ID** block to the **on start** block:

CW01 set MQTT client ID `d:opra53:XinaBox:xb123456`

Connect to the IoT platform/set MQTT broker:

- Add the following block to the **on start** block after **set MQTT client** block:

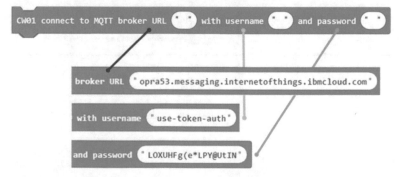

This will connect the weather station to the MQTT broker.

See Table 9-3 for more details.

(*continued*)

Table 9-4. (*continued*)

Step	Description
4	Use the **forever** block.
5	Add a **CW01 send payload** block to the **forever** block:

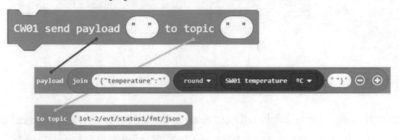

See Table 9-3 for more details.

6	Adapt the join block shown in step 6 to send humidity data:

The rest of the CW01 send payload block remains the same.

| 7 | We have not set up our IoT platform to do anything with the pressure data, so we have nowhere to send it. |

If you have set up a card to display the pressure data, you should try to adapt the code in step 6 and add it here.

Complete the program with a pause to control the rate at which data is transmitted:

Figure 9-21 shows the full **MakeCode** block program.

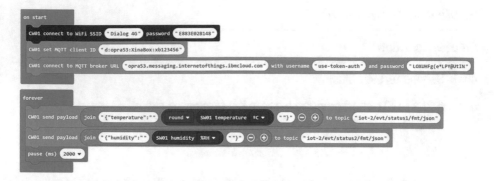

Figure 9-21. *MakeCode blocks for the Wi-Fi weather station*

The full code is available on our **resource website**. You will need to adapt the parameters to work with your IoT Platform, as described in **Table 9-3**.

9.9 Powering and Running the Weather Station

Compile the code and flash it onto your micro:bit. When it has completed flashing remove the USB cable from the micro:bit. We need to power up the weather station in a particular way, as described here:

- Connect the IM01, SW01, and CW01 together. Do NOT connect the micro:bit yet.

- Connect a USB power cable to the IM01 (**Figure 9-22**). Wait until there is a strong blue light showing on the CW01. It should take a few seconds at most.

Figure 9-22. *Step 2 of the powering process*

- Now you can connect your micro:bit to the IM01
  (**Figure 9-23**). On start the micro:bit should display the
  pattern shown. This indicates that the CW01 is trying to
  connect to the Wi-Fi network.

Figure 9-23. *Step 3 of the powering process*

- Once connected to the Wi-Fi network, the letter C is
  shown on the 5X5 LED matrix.

- Next the weather station will try to connect to the IBM
  Watson IoT platform. The diamond pattern on the LED
  matrix indicates an active connection between the
  weather station and the IBM Watson IoT cloud.

Figure 9-24. *The weather station is sending data to the IBM Watson IoT platform*

For as long as the micro:bit is powered and the diamond pattern is showing, data will be sent to the IoT Weather Service. The next section explains how to view the data.

9.10 Viewing the Data Visualizations

With everything running smoothly the micro:bit weather station should be transferring data to the IoT platform. Confirm this by viewing the visualization(s) that you have set up from the pin-board:

- Click **Boards** in the left navigation and then click the **Weather** board created in **Section 9.7** (**Figure 9-25**).

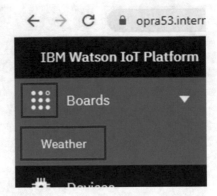

Figure 9-25. *Accessing the line chart to view the data coming from the weather station*

- The line chart will show temperature and humidity data over a time period that you specify (**Figure 9-26**).

Note   The option to publish the board and make it publicly accessible is also available. Under the **Members** tab of **Board settings,** there is an option to **share as read only with everyone**. Checking this box will provide public access to the board via a URL you can share.

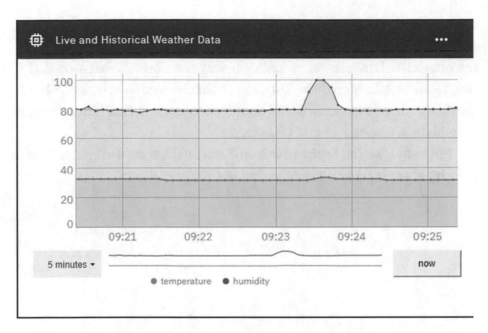

Figure 9-26. *A line chart card on our board showing live and historical weather data*

9.11 Summary

If all has gone to plan, your weather station is hooked up to the IoT platform and you are able to view real-time data on the board using a web browser. At the risk of stating the obvious, you will be able to view the board from anywhere in the world (where you can get an Internet connection). If this seems mundane, bear in mind that 20 years ago this was extremely difficult and even 10, maybe 5, years ago you needed a broad and niche skill set to build something like this.

So take a moment to feel a sense of achievement: what you have done this chapter is not trivial, and only a tiny fraction of the human beings who have ever lived have managed to do this. More importantly, the model we have built is one where we send any sensor data to a cloud service. Switching out different sensors is relatively trivial, which greatly expands the potential of this system. In addition, we used a service that provided a rich set of visualization tools, but what about connecting to other types of service, perhaps even an artificial intelligence service? That is exactly what we will do in **Chapter 11** and **Chapter 12**.

But before we can aspire to use artificial intelligence we need to know a little bit about it, which we will look at in **Chapter 10**.

CHAPTER 10

Introduction to Machine Learning and Artificial Intelligence

HAL 9000[1]: "I'm sorry Dave, I'm afraid I can't do that"

—2001: A Space Odyssey[2]

In this chapter we will look at artificial intelligence (AI) and machine learning (ML) through our data science lens: what are they, how do they differ, and what do they have to offer?

---

[1]**HAL** (Heuristically Programmed ALgorithmic Computer) is an artificial general intelligence computer that controls the systems of the Discovery One spacecraft and interacts with the ship's astronaut crew.

[2]*2001: A Space Odyssey* is a 1968 epic science fiction film produced and directed by Stanley Kubrick. The screenplay was written by Kubrick and Arthur C. Clarke and was inspired by Clarke's short story "The Sentinel" and other short stories by Clarke. – *Wikipedia*

© Philip Meitiner, Pradeeka Seneviratne 2020
P. Meitiner and P. Seneviratne, *Beginning Data Science, IoT, and AI on Single Board Computers*,
https://doi.org/10.1007/978-1-4842-5766-1_10

10.1 Artificial Intelligence

To understand artificial intelligence we first need to understand the real stuff: what is actual intelligence? Do other creatures or machines possess intelligence? Do we, really?

Drawing on our growing understanding of data science, the challenge in trying to answer questions like these objectively, and with any kind of scientific rigor, lies in gathering data about the thing we are studying. And gathering data requires measurement, of some sort. As data scientists, we require a concise and objective definition of "intelligence" and a way to measure it.

But there is no real consensus on what intelligence actually is; no universal definition or handy measuring tool.

The IQ test (Figure 10-1) is the most well-known method for measuring "intelligence." There are other, similar tests as well as some completely different methods, such as calculating the encephalization quotient[3] or an assessment by a trained psychologist.

The problem with the IQ test, and all of the methods at our disposal, is the lack of clarity on what they are trying to measure. The IQ test results correlate with performance on a limited subset of mental skills that were held in high regard by the scientists who created the test. These mental skills were taken to be factors that would correlate strongly with "intelligence".

Perhaps when we finally have a definition of intelligence that everyone agrees on we will observe a correlation with the IQ score. But all we know for sure is that it measures how well someone has performed on a set of tasks. We would question the validity and reliability of extrapolating IQ data and taking it is a straight measure of intelligence.

---

[3]This is basically a measure of the ratio of the size of the brain to the density of the neurons that make it up. Humans have the highest encephalization quotient of all living creatures.

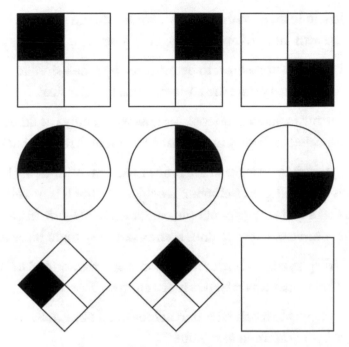

Figure 10-1. *An example IQ test question (from Raven's Progressive Matrices example). What pattern fits in the blank square? Source:* `https://en.wikipedia.org/wiki/Intelligence_quotient#/` `media/File:Raven_Matrix.svg`

It does seem inevitable that this IQ is not the same as the intelligence that separate us from slugs or trees. It is THAT intelligence that is the holy grail of computer scientists, and the people that finance them.

Despite the fact that the term intelligence is nebulous, we have little difficulty identifying **intelligent behavior** in other people and by nonhuman entities (e.g., a dolphin, chimpanzee, or computer).

Intelligent behaviors are actions that:

- An observer would not attribute to luck or to mirroring learned behavior.

- Are not reflexes or automatic responses: they required volition and insight from the party displaying the behavior.

- Result in an outcome that is favorable to the entity, or the avoidance of an unpleasant outcome.

- We would not expect to be repeated by other, similar entities every time the circumstance are identical.

- Are not isolated incidents. An intelligent entity would be expected to display intelligent behavior on a regular basis.

We can therefore observe intelligence in action. Admittedly labeling an action as an **intelligent behavior** is subjective, but it is possible to list behaviors that a wide range of people would agree meet the threshold for **intelligent behavior**. For machines some examples might be as follows:

- It displayed a behavior that it was not programmed to display that was effective in meeting an objective.

- It displayed a behavior that achieved an objective it was not programmed to pursue.

Focusing on intelligent behavior gives us a practical way to define intelligence:

- Intelligence is the impetus that prompts an organism or machine to demonstrate "intelligent behavior."

In a wonderful case of irony, Forrest Gump got it right when he said "stupid is as stupid does"; for us that translates into "intelligence is performing intelligent behavior." It sounds better the way he says it though.

10.2 AI/ML?

The terms machine learning (ML) and artificial intelligence (AI) are encountered frequently in the press and social media, but few of us are clear on the distinction. At the risk of annoying experts by oversimplifying, the key difference between AI and ML can be summed up as follows:

- **AI** is concerned with creating machines that display **intelligent behavior**.

- The core goal of **ML** is data analysis. It is a branch of AI that focuses on systems that can learn and improve from experience: enhancing the quality and accuracy of the outcomes they produce or finding new and novel ways to reach an outcome.

ML is a subset of AI, and the example we look at later in the book is an ML implementation.

To illustrate the difference between AI and ML consider this: when AlphaGo beat the world's best player at the board game Go it was a triumph of ML. It would be a triumph of AI if AlphaGo decided to deliberately lose a game to avoid being detected, or to ensure its human opponent did not get too upset.

We are not going to look at each of the 14 different types of learning that compromise ML. Neither are we going to ponder the three or four different types of AI or probe exactly what is, and isn't, ML. The core elements that comprise AI are fascinating, but again we will pass. Our goal here is to foster an intuitive understanding of AI and learn how to use it as a tool for data science experimentation.

10.3 ML/AI and Data Science

The field of AI is vast and complicated; we can barely hope to scratch the surface in a single chapter. But scratching the surface is all we need to be able to use AI in our data science work – in the same way that we can drive a car without building it from scratch, so we can use AI services in our data science endeavors without knowing how to build an AI model ourselves.

There are a large range of AI services that are available for public use, and many of those are transactional: data is passed into the service, some activity is undertaken using the data, and some data is returned. It's quite mundane really.

Using a service requires no real knowledge of what actually goes on within the service: how it manipulates and transforms our data is a "black box." Nevertheless, as was the case with sensors, to use these services effectively a basic understanding of what they do with our data is ideal. In the next section we undertake an exercise that will help us understand how an ML service operates.

There is a lot of hype about what AI is capable of and what the future holds for it. But make no mistake, the cleverest AI does not have a patch on you as far as being able to undertake novel and intuitive cognitive leaps. The edge that AI has over us resides in its ability to crunch numbers: to work with mind-boggling huge sets of data and to perform a staggering volume of analysis on that data.

AI is a very powerful tool for sophisticated data science applications, but without a human being somewhere in the process an AI is little more than an infernal machine – a robot dog forever chasing its own tail. AI is like the chef, using all manner of ingredients to serve its human masters with perfectly prepared meals, but the chef is unable to taste its own creations. Ultimately it is humans who will look at any facts/conclusions generated by an AI and will make the most important judgment: is this interesting?

One of the pivotal moments for AI in the twentieth century was when IBM's Deep Blue supercomputer (Figure 10-2) beat grandmaster and world number 1 Gary Kasparov at chess, in May 1997. The computer won 3.5/2.5 in a six game series, and for many this felt like the beginning of the end of human intellectual dominance. Forevermore would computers be "better" than humans at chess – what next?

But there is more to the story: Kasparov put forward a strong case arguing that something untoward occurred (he used the term "cheating"). He presented a few arguments in support; the most interesting was one particular move that Deep Blue made that Kasparov was adamant an AI would not be capable of formulating. Deep Blue had several human operators who worked on it while the game was being played, so the means to interfere existed. Fuel was given to Kasparov's claims when IBM refused his demands for a rematch and dismantled Deep Blue. Whatever the truth is, this battle between human and AI was big news and the success of Deep Blue signaled a new era: AI had arrived.

Figure 10-2. IBM's Deep Blue, at the Computer History Museum.
`https://commons.m.wikimedia.org/wiki/File:Deep_Blue.`
`jpg#mw-jump-to-license`

10.4 Thinking Like a Machine

It is often said that the best way to understand someone is to walk a mile in their shoes. By extension, to understand ML it makes sense to perform some of the sorts of functions that a machine learning service undertakes.

We are going to build an experiment that requires us to go through a number of steps in the data analysis process. The experiment is designed to investigate a target behavior and see if there are any correlations with a set of environmental data that we will capture.

The real point of the experiment is not the results per se, but the style of analysis they will allow us to undertake. A lot of what we do during the experiment can be done by an AI, and quite a bit can't. By considering these side-by-side we will gain insights into what AI brings to the table.

Despite this, the experiment we suggest does have the potential to yield interesting data too. The key is choosing the right target behavior:

What is it that makes you decide to get up and make a drink? Or lean back in your chair and stretch? Or scratch the back of your head? Machines don't really display comparable behavioral traits, or "quirks".

Are these sometimes random, sometimes pointless, and sometimes even automatic actions evidence of the elusive intelligence we seek? Or is it possible that some environmental stimulus triggers these responses in you?

Pick a target behavior carefully and strap in: the experiment could reveal insights into the age-old dilemma between fate and free will (spoiler: it probably won't).

10.5 Experimental Design

Table 10-1 outlines the activities we will undertake to investigate the impact of environmental conditions on a target behavior.

Table 10-1. *Investigating factors that trigger a target behavior*

Exercise 10.1	**Do environmental factors trigger a target behavior?**
Summary	We will record environmental conditions that are present when a target behavior is exhibited. We will then look at these environmental measures and see if there is a correlation with the target behavior.
Step-by-step process	1. Decide on a target behavior to investigate.
	2. Build the data gathering instrument described in the Hardware section and flash on the appropriate code.
	3. Find a suitable location for the data gathering instrument.
	4. Place the instrument in the chosen location and power it up.
	5. Leave the device running. When the target behavior is displayed, click B on the micro:bit.
	6. Once you have 6 instances of the behavior, extract the data and load it onto a laptop/computer.
	7. Use software on your laptop/computer to undertake the analysis outlined in the Analysis section.
What we will learn	• Is there evidence that any of the environmental factors might play a role in triggering the target behavior?
	• The value of an AI service might add to an experiment of this nature.

The experiment has two distinct steps:

1. The data collection phase

2. The data analysis phase

The target behavior I used is **the impetus to make a cup of coffee**, which I feel two to three times every day while working at my desk. There is no time-based pattern: I don't have a cup at a given time every day or at specific intervals. Instead, I find myself drifting toward the kitchen, often without having made a conscious decision to actually make another cup. For me this is a very suitable example, but you will need to find one that is meaningful to you.

10.6 Hardware Requirements

The components that our digital instrument will need to include are shown in **Figure 10-3**.

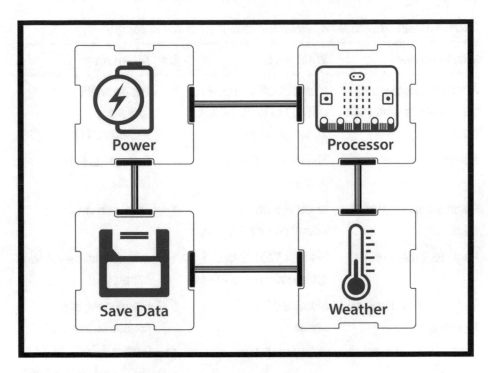

Figure 10-3. *Core components of a data logger*

Table 10-2 lists the specific hardware that we will use to build our data logger (or "target behavior monitoring instrument").

Table 10-2. *Hardware requirements for the data logger*

What you need	What we use	Qty	Alternatives
A microprocessor and the means to flash code onto it	micro:bit with micro-B USB cable to connect to laptop/desktop	1	Raspberry Pi Arduino XinaBox CS11
Power	The micro:bit battery holder	1	Seenov Inc Solar Battery
A sensor to read weather data	XinaBox SW01 – advanced weather sensor	1	SparkFun Weatherbit
Persistent memory	Xinabox IM01 micro:bit bridge with microSD card	1	microprocessor onboard memory
The means to connect it all together	XinaBox IM01 micro:bit bridge	1	Breadboard, edge connector breakout, crocodile/alligator leads, and hookup wires
	xBus connectors	1	

Before using the microSD card make sure it is formatted using the FAT32 option. If you are unsure how to format an SD card, the process is explained on our **resource website**.

When you have formatted it, insert the microSD card into the slot on the back of the IM01.

The data logging tool described in the **What we use** column is shown in **Figure 10-4**.

Figure 10-4. *Assembled hardware for data logging*

10.7 Software

It is possible to write software for the micro:bit that will use the onboard memory to record the data we are looking at: the code and techniques described in **Chapter 4** will serve this purpose. Memory limitations on the micro:bit will severely limit the amount of data we can collect though.

223

Alternately a Raspberry Pi, Arduino, or CS11 core from XinaBox will be able to support the data logging app required. There are also other solutions that can be used to extract data from a micro:bit, such as the Excel Data Streamer. Whatever technique you use to capture sensor data will be adequate as long as you can tag the moment in time that the target behavior is observed.

We use the combination of the micro:bit and the XinaBox IM01 bridge as it is perfect for our needs and very simple to use. The code we use will record a range of different sensor readings and will write these to a CSV file. This file is saved on the microSD card that is mounted on the IM01 bridge.

The coding element is not central to what we are looking at in this chapter: we are not introducing any new coding concepts, just employing concepts we've already covered (saving sensor data to persistent memory). The software required can be downloaded from our resource website, which also shows how to replicate the code in MakeCode using the IM01:

Go to `http://xib.one/XB` and search for **Section 10.7**.

10.8 Using the Hardware

When the hardware has been constructed, it can be powered up and used. **Figure 10-5** shows some snapshots of our hardware in action.

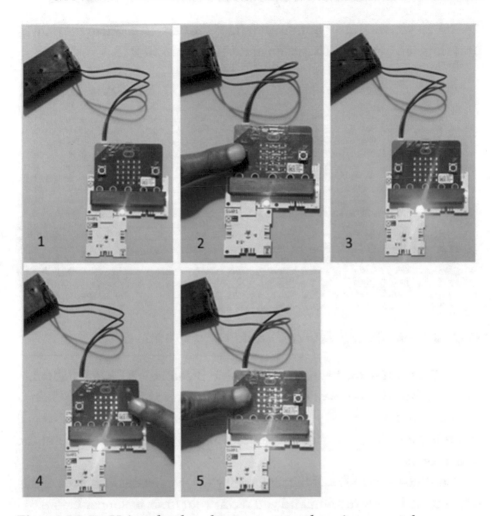

Figure 10-5. *Using the data logger to record environmental conditions that are present when a target behavior is exhibited. (1) Powering up. (2) Pressing button A to start recording. (3) Data is recording. (4) Pressing the button B to tag the data. (5) Pressing button A again to stop/resume recording*

Click the A button on the micro:bit to start it recording and leave it somewhere within reach. Act as you normally would until you notice that you have exhibited the target behavior. At this point click the B button.

When you click the B button, you "tag" the data: a record in the data file is labeled with a "1". This is illustrated in **Figure 10-6**.

	A	B	C	D	E	F	G	H	I	J	K
1	Time	Acc X	Acc Y	Acc Z	Mag X	Mag Y	Mag Z	**B**	Temp	Pressure	Humidity
2	4195	0.007812	-0.339822	-0.874944	-56.700001	85.800003	-31.9	0	27.450001	989.390015	38.354492
3	4346	-0.01953	-0.382788	-0.867132	-56.599998	85.400002	-30.799999	0	27.450001	989.369995	38.342773
4	4498	0	-0.359352	-0.921816	-56	86.199997	-30.4	0	27.440001	989.390015	38.300781
5	4651	0.031248	-0.261702	-0.999936	-58	84.300003	-32.299999	0	27.440001	989.369995	38.395508
6	4820	0.11718	-0.35154	-0.890568	-61.599998	80.599998	-32.5	0	27.440001	989.400024	38.448242
7	4972	0.09765	-0.210924	-0.941346	-62.299999	79.599998	-33.400002	0	27.440001	989.380005	38.458984
8	5124	0.023436	-0.207018	-0.89638	-63.700001	78	-34.299999	0	27.440001	989.340027	38.46875
9	5277	0.070308	-0.246078	-0.984312	-61.799999	75.400002	-35.700001	0	27.440001	989.340027	38.532227
10	5446	0.031248	-0.23436	-0.910098	-65.300003	76.300003	-33.700001	0	27.450001	989.380005	38.449219
11	5599	0.433566	-0.320292	-0.828072	-70.699997	80.300003	-29.4	0	27.440001	989.400024	38.510742
12	5752	0.277326	-0.359352	-0.960876	-70.900002	83.800003	-27	1	27.440001	989.369995	38.594727
13	5905	0.167958	-0.304668	-0.757764	-70.599998	84.5	-25.9	0	27.440001	989.380005	38.658203
14	6075	0.308574	-0.31248	-0.992124	-72.5	82	-26.1	0	27.440001	989.369995	38.805664
15	6228	0.15624	-0.269514	-0.95697	-72.400002	80.199997	-27.200001	0	27.43	989.369995	38.743164
16	6382	0.304668	-0.320292	-0.960876	-74.099998	77.800003	-27.5	0	27.43	989.380005	38.827148
17	6669	0.269514	-0.296856	-0.910098	-74	77.800003	-26.299999	0	27.42	989.349976	38.709961
18	6822	0.23436	-0.367164	-0.890568	-72.800003	76.900002	-28.9	0	27.4	989.369995	38.583008

Figure 10-6. *Tagged data collected in the experiment*

In **Figure 10-6** the header for column H (heading = **B**) is highlighted. Note that row 12 has the value **1** in this column (also highlighted). When you click the B button on your micro:bit, the value 1 is written into this column. This allows us to identify a point in time when the target behavior was observed.

Continue to record and tag data until you have several instances of the target behavior. We recommend you record four to six instances before moving on to the analysis phase; more instances will yield better results but will require more work.

10.9 Analyzing the Data

Once you have collected and downloaded the data, the next step is to analyze it and see whether any interesting secrets are buried in its depths.

If you have used the hardware and software suggested earlier, you should have a data set with the following labels:

- **Timestamp**: This is an integer that is a measure of how many milliseconds have elapsed since the micro:bit was powered up.

- **Acc X**: A measure of acceleration in the x-plane (relative to the micro:bit and recorded from the onboard accelerometer).

- **Acc Y**: A measure of acceleration in the y-plane.

- **Acc Z**: A measure of acceleration in the z-plane.

- **Mag X**: A measure of magnetic attraction in the x-plane (recorded by the micro:bit's onboard magnetometer).

- **Mag Y**: A measure of magnetic attraction in the y-plane.

- **Mag Z**: A measure of magnetic attraction in the z-plane.

- **B**: Tags – the value is 0 except when the B button is clicked.

- **Temp**: Temperature in Centigrade recorded by the SW01 xChip.

- **Pressure**: Atmospheric pressure recorded by the SW01 xChip.

- **Humidity**: Relative humidity recorded by the SW01 xChip.

The data in the field labeled **B** tells us when the subject exhibited a target behavior.

A fairly simple way to look for correlations between fields of data and the target behavior is to draw line charts using the process described here:

- Locate a point in the data where the target behavior was exhibited – where the value 1 appears in column H.

227

- Choose one of the other data fields to look at
  (e.g., temperature). Highlight data in that field from
  the current record UPWARD (to select data recorded
  before the target behavior was tagged): select a few
  hundred records.

- Click **Insert/Chart/Line Chart**. Create a line chart
  showing the highlighted data.

- Your chart will look something like Figure 10-7.

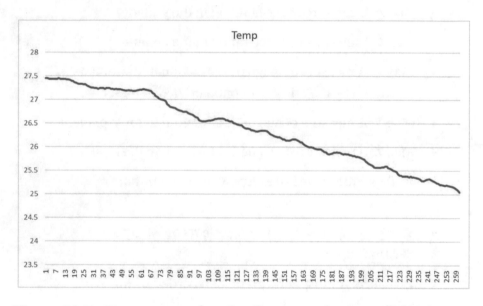

Figure 10-7. *Temperature data leading up to the target behavior*

What we are looking at in **Figure 10-7** is temperature data. It shows
data from a couple of minutes before I found myself feeling the urge to
make a cup of coffee. I could have taken a much bigger chunk of data
over a longer period of time, but I chose not to: the urge to make coffee is
typically quite sudden, so I wanted to look at a short time period. Use your
logic in a similar way to choose a time period to consider.

By itself, this visualization is of little value. We need to look at other, similar graphs and check if there are similar patterns. Repeat the process of generating charts for each instance of the target behavior. Try to use the same number of data points and don't let the chart use overlapping data.

I generated four charts, shown in **Figure 10-8**.

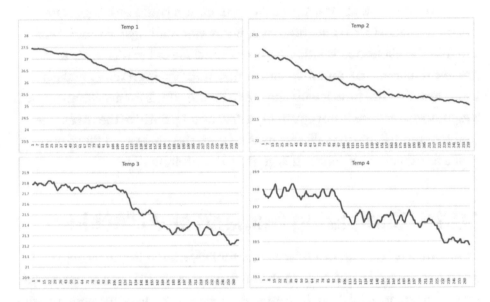

Figure 10-8. *Four charts showing temperature leading up to my target behavior*

Looking at these charts side-by-side helps us see if there is a pattern: similarities in the shapes leading up to the target behavior.

In the four instances shown there is a steady decline in the temperature up to the moment I felt the urge to make a cuppa. This was unexpected: although I hypothesized that the most likely measure to correlate with the target behavior was the temperature, I did not really expect to see a pattern. This data does not prove anything, but it shows me that temperature might play a role in triggering my coffee-impulse. The data scientist in me marks this result as something worth investigating more rigorously later.

The next step in our analysis is to repeat this for all the different measures and see if any other patterns emerge. There are nine sensor readings we can choose from so lots of charting to do – better get started!

But, **no**. At this point we apply our human intelligence to guide our analysis:

Is there any likelihood at all that acceleration could be a trigger for my target behavior? What about magnetometer readings? My logic tells me that the likelihood is either zero, or very close to zero. There is a greater likelihood of humidity and/or pressure playing a role. I make a judgment that the time it will take me to create charts for acceleration and magnetometer data is not worth my effort and I prioritize the measures that feel more likely to yield results. And with the time saved I'll go and make another cup of coffee (it is getting a bit chilly)!

10.10 Comparing Humans and Machines

There are a broad range of AI services publicly available and we will look at how to access one of these in the next chapter. In this experiment we did everything manually though. **Table 10-3** lists a number of the activities and actions we undertook and gives an idea of what an AI might be capable of doing in each instance.

Table 10-3. *Data analysis: comparing how a human and an AI might undertake the analysis outlined here*

What I did	What AI would do
I designed an experiment to investigate something because I was curious.	An AI will react to a command of some kind. They are not innately curious.
I chose to look at temperature first: it felt like the most likely measure to have an impact.	AI would look at all the different measures and then look at all sorts of combinations of them. Over time it would learn to prioritize measures that more consistently yield significant results.
I made 4 charts that all looked at a similar time period which I chose based on logical assumptions. I then visually inspected the charts I had made.	AI would use a broad range of pattern matching algorithms to analyze the data thoroughly, testing all sorts of different time segments. With enough time to process the data it would find any statistically significant results.
I looked for patterns.	An AI looks for patterns.
I used logic to cut down on my workload. I valued my time and left out measures I felt were spurious.	An AI would use prior learning to target how it searches, and will continue working as long as there is work to do, or until it is told to stop.
I decided that the results were interesting and potentially worth investigating further.	An AI would report on results that had some degree of statistical significance. We could train an AI to assign a score to the likelihood that a human would find a result interesting.
I might make some predictions based on intuition and experience.	An AI might make predictions based on a vast body of prior, similar events and a highly trained and evolved prediction model.

Notice how the activities in **Table 10-3** that are most likely to qualify as "intelligent behavior" are listed in the **What I did** column. AI has a great deal to offer, but the real intelligence in data science still comes from the people involved in the process.

What is clear though is the value of AI to perform volumes of sophisticated analysis that would be too time-consuming for a person, and beyond the skill set of most of us. In the following chapter we will unlock this power and begin to use AI in our data science work.

10.11 Summary

In this chapter we looked at intelligence, both artificial and real, and learned what lies at the core of AI and ML. We then undertook an experiment that gathered data which we analyzed: the experiment was designed to make us process data in ways that could be compared to AI.

The key takeout is that AI is a tool which can be added to human intellect to achieve outcomes a human could not on their own. Conversely without a human intellect to drive it, most AI services are as relevant as the sound a tree makes when it falls where no one can hear it.

We have no evidence yet that AI can help us become better data scientists, but it clearly has the potential to. It is time to use it.

CHAPTER 11

Using ML Services

In **Chapter 9** we saw how to connect our micro:bit weather station to an IoT platform for the purpose of enhancing our data science toolkit. In **Chapter 10** we considered the potential value that AI/ML can bring to our data science experimentation, how it can liberate us from elements of the process and allow us to maximize the time available to exercise our curiosity and intuition – the irreplaceable human traits that are the true brains of data science.

In this chapter we will bring both of these together and look at how an online and free-to-use ML service can be added to our growing weather station project: we are going to build a genuine "artificial intelligence powered predictive weather station."

11.1 Defining Our IoT Application

What is an "Artificial intelligence powered predictive weather station"? What exactly are we going to build? The requirements are simple to describe:

1. It includes an edge device: a micro:bit recording temperature and humidity data and sending it to an IoT platform.

© Philip Meitiner, Pradeeka Seneviratne 2020

P. Meitiner and P. Seneviratne, *Beginning Data Science, IoT, and AI on Single Board Computers*, https://doi.org/10.1007/978-1-4842-5766-1_11

2. It will use AI (ML specifically) to analyze that data and make predictions about the likelihood of rain based on it.

3. Predictions will be shown on the micro:bit 5x5 LED display.

We are familiar by now with items 1 and 3 in the list; in this chapter we will focus on 2: how to integrate an ML service into our weather station. The process is nontrivial: we are going to have to build an **IoT application**.

The term **IoT application** is used in this chapter to collectively describe all the different IoT services that we set up and use and the functionality that they jointly provide. It is appropriate to call it an application: what we are doing is using a range of modules ("services") and configuring them to deliver an outcome. This is similar to using several different blocks of code together to make a program, or connecting a few electronic components together to make a digital instrument. In many respects the weather prediction example we are building here is the Hello World! of ML in physical computing.

This chapter focuses on building the IoT application. The edge device that we build – our weather station instrument – is covered in **Chapter 12**. It is useful to remember that you could send data to the IoT application from any viable source, not just the one we will build in the next chapter.

11.2 Choosing an IoT Service Provider

A fundamental component of the IoT application we are building is the ML engine that will power our predictive model. Before we can start building our application we need to find a suitable ML service to use.

We will use Microsoft Azure. We chose to use Azure, rather than extend the IBM IoT Platform we built in **Chapter 9**, for a number of reasons:

1. Variety. Knowing how to use two of the leading IoT service providers is better than just one. And perhaps one is blocked or doesn't work for you.

2. Setting up an IoT platform is slightly different for each provider. Once you have set up both an IBM and an Azure platform, you should have more confidence setting up any IoT platform.

3. Through Azure we can access a broad and growing range of services to add to our toolkit.

   Once you have worked through this chapter, we encourage you to go back to your IBM IoT Platform and look at how that can be integrated with the IBM Watson AI services.

The process of setting Azure up is quite long and onerous, but once complete you can reuse most of the functionality and switch out bits like the data you send and the ML service you use. Although we focus on the weather station, you should be able to use the same process to integrate different edge devices with a broad range of the ML services available through Azure.

11.3 Setting Up Microsoft Azure: Cloud Computing Services

The first thing you need is an **Azure** subscription; if you don't have one, you should be able to create a **free 30-day** account which will grant you access to all the services used here.

There are two steps to get things started:

1. Set up a Microsoft Azure account: search online for "set up an Azure account" to find out how to set one up where you are located.

2. Once you have set up your Azure account, ensure you have access to Azure Machine Learning Studio (https://studio.azureml.net/).

11.4 Creating an IoT Hub Using Azure Portal

This section describes how to create an **IoT hub** using the Azure portal.

An **IoT hub** is the name given to a service that links the edge devices (in this case our weather station, but we could have multiple devices) with the IoT application. It controls access of the devices to the IoT application.

To set up the hub, you will need to do the following:

- Sign in to the Azure portal (https://portal.azure.com/).

- From the Azure home page, select the **+ Create a resource** button.

- Enter **IoT hub** in the **Search the Marketplace** field.

- In the **Marketplace** page, select **IoT hub** from the search results.

- In the **IoT hub** page, select **Create**.

- On the **Basics** tab, complete the fields as follows:

Subscription:	Select the subscription to use for your hub (e.g., *Pay-As-You-Go*).
Resource Group:	Select **Create new** and fill in the name you want to use (e.g., *iot-hubs*), and then select **OK**.
Region:	Select the region from the list in which you want your hub to be located. Select the location closest to you, but if your area is not available, use the default shown.
IoT hub Name:	Enter a name for your hub (e.g., *your-iot-hub*). This name must be globally unique. If the name you enter is available, a green checkmark appears. To keep the uniqueness, we used the ISBN-13 number of this book which is 978-1484243565.

- Once completed, your **Basics** tab should look something like this (**Figure 11-1**).

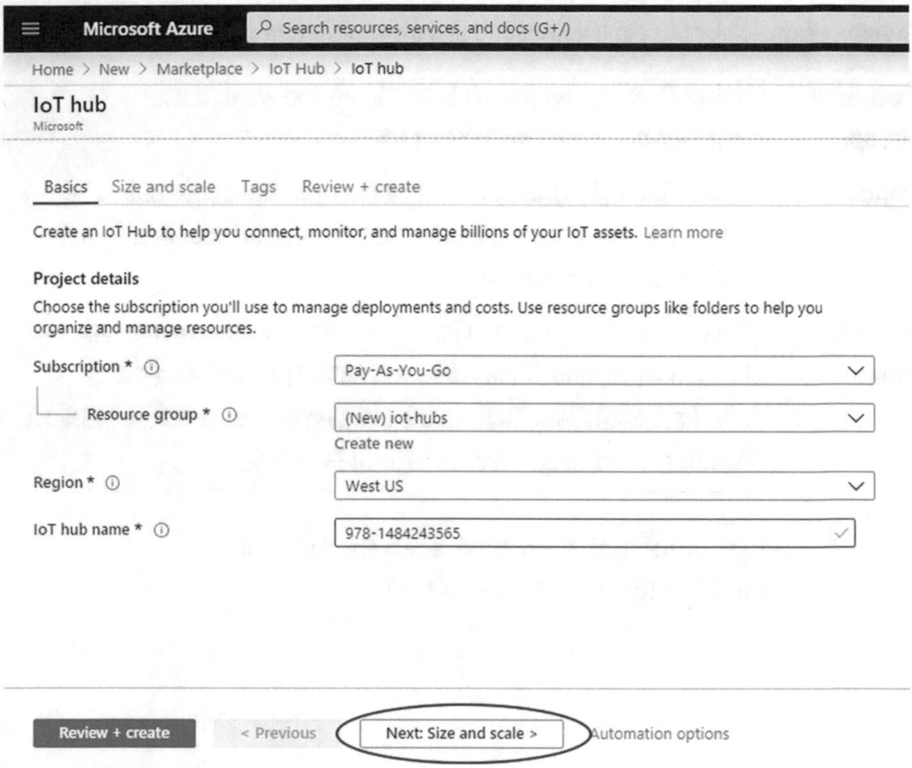

Figure 11-1. *Configuring the Basics tab*

- Select **Next: Size and scale** to continue creating your hub.
  On the **Size and scale** tab, complete the fields as follows:

Pricing and scale tier:	Choose F1: Free tier
	NOTE: Free IoT hubs are limited to one per subscription.
IoT Hub units:	1
Azure Security Center:	Off
Advanced Settings > Device-to-cloud partitions:	Keep the default value 4

Once completed, your **Size and scale** tab should look something like this (**Figure 11-2**).

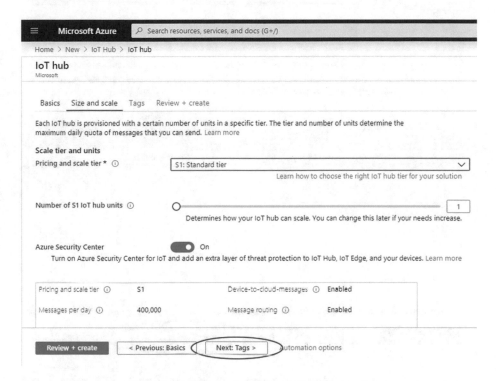

Figure 11-2. Configuring the Size and scale tab

- Select **Next: Tags** to continue creating your hub. On the **Tags** tab, complete the fields as follows:

Name:	department
Value:	data science

- Once completed, your **Tags** tab should look something like this (**Figure 11-3**).

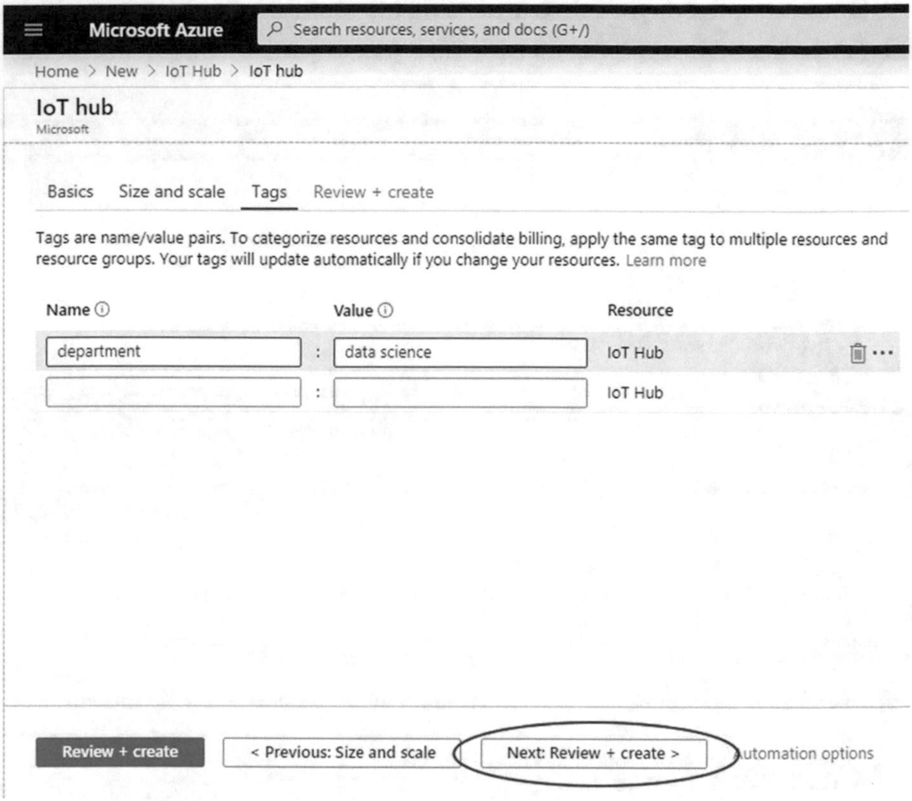

Figure 11-3. *Configuring the Tags tab*

- Select **Next: Review + create** to continue creating your
  hub. Your **Review + create** tab should look something
  like this (**Figure 11-4**).

Figure 11-4. *Review + create tab*

- Select **Create** to create your new hub. Creating the hub may take a few minutes.

After creating the IoT hub we'll delve into the Azure Machine Learning Studio and will set up an Azure Logic App. You will need to provide the name of the **IoT hub** and the **Resource group** when you create the Logic App, so make sure you have these details available.

11.5 Setting Up a Weather Prediction Model in Azure Machine Learning Studio

To use a weather prediction model we first choose one: there are several options available. Then we have to import the chosen "weather prediction experiment" into our Azure Machine Learning Studio project:

- Open ML Studio – check that you are signed in.

- In a separate tab in the same browser, go to this URL (https://gallery.azure.ai/Experiment/Weather-prediction-model-1) to locate the weather prediction AI "experiment" that we use. *There are several available that you could also try, as well as loads of other experiments to play with.*

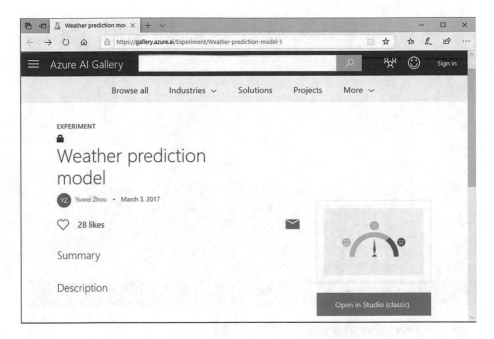

Figure 11-5. *Azure AI Gallery experiment: Weather prediction model*

- Click **Open in Studio**. A modal window will then pop up prompting you to choose a region: leave the default option and click the tick to continue.

- Once the experiment has imported, the ML Studio interface should look something like this (**Figure 11-6**).

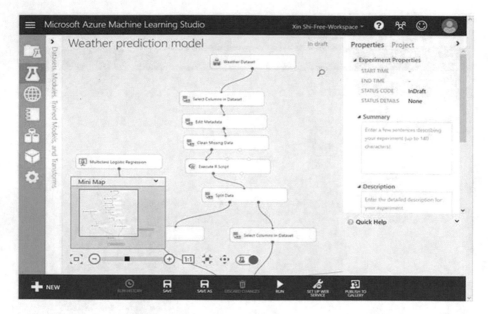

Figure 11-6. *Weather prediction model*

- Click **RUN** (in the menu at the bottom of the screen) to validate the steps.

- As each step in the process runs, it also validates, and you will see a green tick get added as each validates successfully. There shouldn't be any errors. It should stop running once all steps have been validated – it may take a minute or so.

- Click **SETUP WEB SERVICE ➤ Predictive Web Service.** This can be found in the bottom menu next to **RUN**.

Note   The SETUP WEB SERVICE option won't be selectable unless the system has run all the way through the validation process in the previous step. When complete, all the steps should show little green ticks.

- After you click to set up the web service, your view updates as a new version of the model is generated: the **Predictive Experiment,** which is what we will use. Once complete there should be two tabs: Training Experiment and Predictive Experiment.

- We are going to **MOVE** the **Web services input** block. This block tells the experiment where to inject the data from the web service (i.e., from our weather station instrument) into the model.

- Click the line joining **Web services input** to **Weather Dataset** (click where it joins the **Web services input** block) – this will disconnect them.

- Now connect the line to the **Score Model** block as shown in **Figure 11-7**.

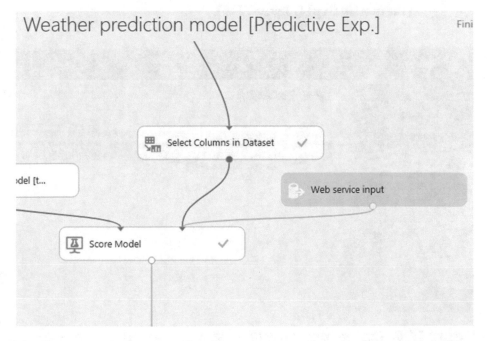

Figure 11-7. *Connecting "Web service input" to the "Score Model"*

- Once you have completed these, click **RUN** to let the new model validate. Remember to wait for it to complete.

- Click **DEPLOY WEB SERVICE** to deploy the model as a web service.

You have now built an **experiment** which you can see by clicking the **Experiments** list on the left-hand menu. You have also created a **Web Service** object which we will link to from Azure: we will pass data into this Web Service. To do so we need to take note of a couple of details (URI and API Key):

- Click the **Web Services** link on the left-hand menu. You will see a list showing at least one web service.

- Click the name of the web service we just created – by default it will be named **Weather prediction model (Predictive Exp) (Figure 11-8)**.

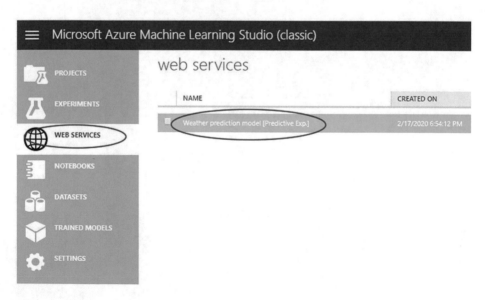

Figure 11-8. *Link for accessing the details of the web service*

- In the **weather prediction model [predictive exp.]** page, make a note of your API Key listed (**Figure 11-9**).

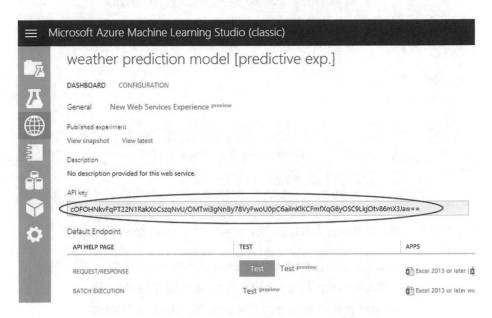

Figure 11-9. *The API key for the Web Service authentication*

- In the **weather prediction model [predictive exp.]** page, click the **REQUEST/RESPONSE** link (seen toward the bottom left in **Figure 11-9**).

- A new tab should open with a page titled **Request Response API Documentation for Weather prediction model [Predictive Exp.]**. This has the final detail we'll need to use in Azure: make note of the **Request URI** from this page (**Figure 11-10**).

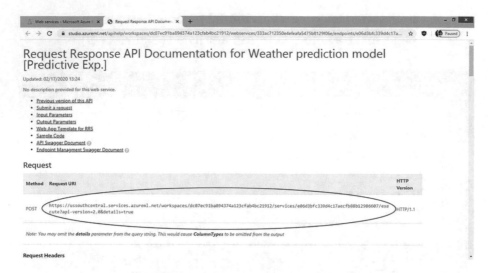

Figure 11-10. *Request URI for the weather prediction model*

- Now switch to the **weather prediction model [predictive exp.]** page (in a separate tab) again. Then test the web service by clicking the **Test** button (**Figure 11-11**).

Figure 11-11. *Test link for the web service*

- You should be prompted to add dummy variables for temperature and humidity: enter some values and then click the **OK** button (tick) (**Figure 11-12**).

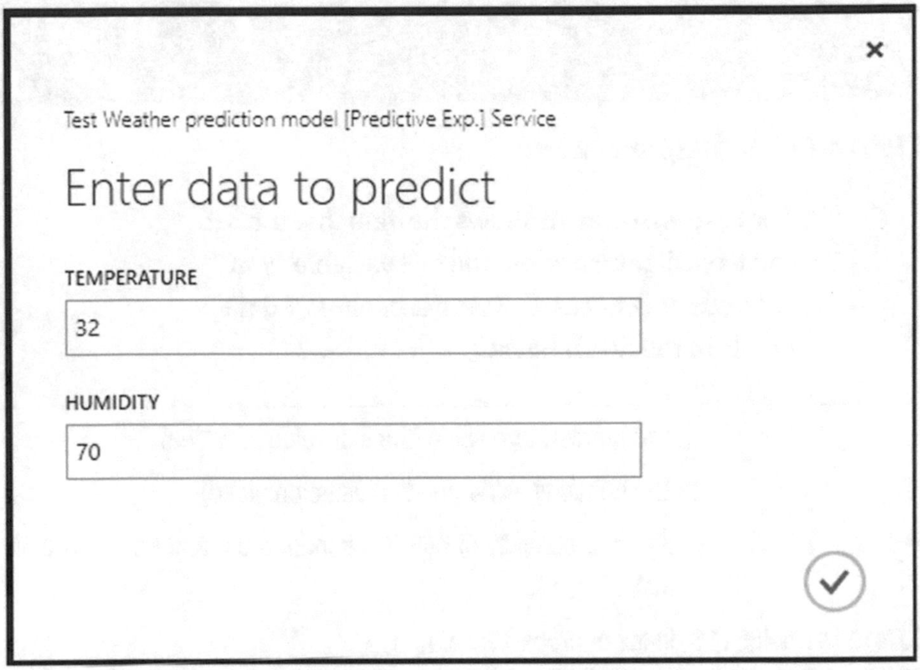

Test Weather prediction model [Predictive Exp.] Service

Enter data to predict

TEMPERATURE

32

HUMIDITY

70

Figure 11-12. *Input modal box for entering temperature and humidity values manually*

- The predicted result will display just above the bottom menu. Click **DETAILS** to view the full result. It should look similar to **Figure 11-13**.

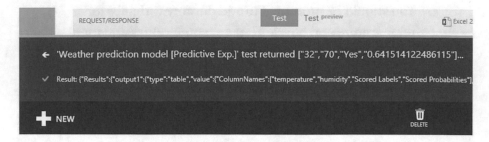

Figure 11-13. *Response result*

The **response result** shows the data that the ML
service will return when the test variables you
entered are processed. There are four key data
points in the result (array):

32	The temperature value (the test value provided)
70	The humidity value (the test value provided)
Yes	Binary probability of rain: Yes if index >0.5 and No if less than that
0.641514122486115	Index of probability of rain

- **CLOSE** the result section.

    The test should work fine. If not try deleting the
    web service and deploying again, or importing the
    experiment again.

Azure Machine Learning Studio is set up and ready to go. Before
our IoT application is complete, we need to define how the services we
are using will all work together and how the data will be passed from
each component of our application to the next: we need to set up the
workflow.

11.6 Creating a Workflow Using Azure Logic Apps

Let's take stock of what we have done so far:

1. We set up an account with **Azure** to access its cloud services.

2. We configured an **IoT hub** so that we could communicate data between Azure and our weather station.

3. We launched **Azure ML Studio**, chose a weather prediction model, and then set it up ready to use.

So far there are three separate components/services that we need to get to work together: our weather station instrument, our IoT Hub, and the ML Studio model/experiment. A more sophisticated experiment than this may have multiple data sources and may use a variety of services/add-ons. Workflow tools are used to help manage complex projects with lots of moving parts: in essence they ensure that steps are undertaken in the right sequence.

In this section we build a workflow using **Azure Logic Apps**. This app will regularly check to see if data is being sent from our weather station. When new data is detected, this app sends it to the weather prediction model (hosted on Azure ML Studio) through a web service. It will also receive responses from the ML service, convert (**parse**) them to a format we specify, and then send the result back to our weather station device.

Follow the steps listed here to create a new logic app:

- From the Azure home page, under **Azure services**, click **Create a resource**.

- On the **New** page, under **Azure Marketplace**, click **Integration** and then click **Logic App** (**Figure 11-14**).

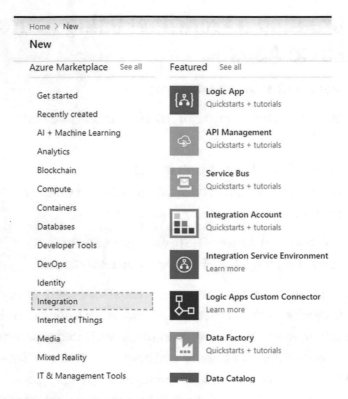

Figure 11-14. *Selecting Logic App resource*

- On the **Logic App** pane, provide details about your
  logic app as shown in **Figure 11-15**. After you're done,
  click **Review + Create** to validate your details.

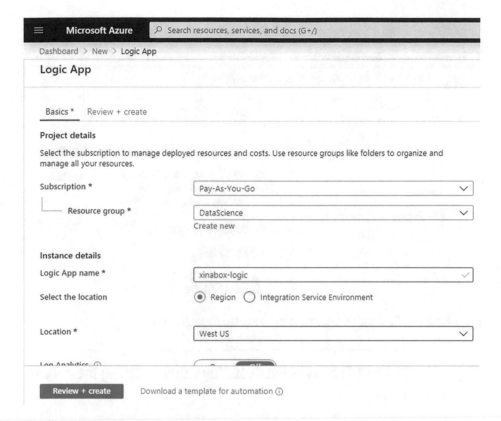

Figure 11-15. *Details of the Basics tab*

- If the information you provided is correct, click **Create**. This will start to deploy your logic app. This may take a few moments.

- Click **Go to resource** for your deployed logic app (**Figure 11-16**).

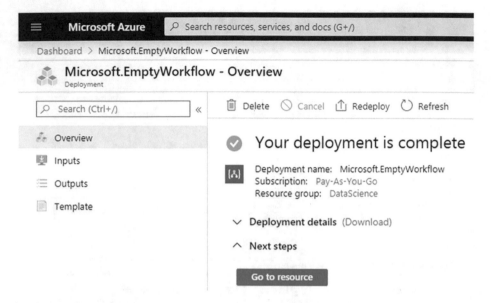

Figure 11-16. *Deployment confirmation message*

Tip   You can also find and select your logic app by typing the name in the search box.

- The **Logic Apps Designer** opens and shows a page with an introduction video and commonly used triggers.

- Scroll down the page. Under **Templates**, click **Blank Logic App**.

11.7 Setting Up the workflow

We will now review the workflow that we have just created and will ensure each step is configured properly.

There are five basic actions/steps/events that are managed by the Azure Logic App and which are key to the workflow; whatever service you use to implement ML, there will be an equivalent to each of these steps:

1. Sending data from the weather station instrument

2. Passing the data into the ML service

3. Interpreting ("parsing") results from the ML service

4. Setting up a variable to store the data from the ML service

5. Managing and sending this data back to the weather station instrument

We will review each of these steps in more detail.

Step 1: Sending Data from the Weather Station Instrument

The workflow begins/is triggered when data is sent from the weather station instrument. This step is referred to as the **When a http request is received** trigger in the Azure Logic app.

To set up this part of the workflow:

- In the **Logic App Designer**, under the **search box**, select **All**.

- In the search box, enter **http** to find the HTTP triggers.

- From the **Triggers** list, click **When a http request is received** trigger (**Figure 11-17**).

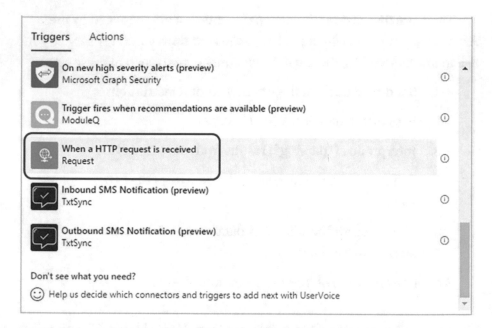

Figure 11-17. *Choosing "When a HTTP request is received"*
trigger

- Provide the information for the **When a http request
  is received** trigger as shown in **Figure 11-18**.

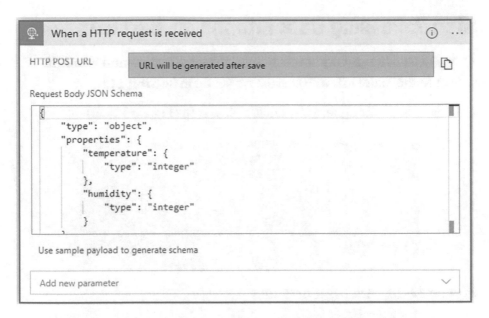

Figure 11-18. *"When a http request is received" trigger details*

- The following is the full listing of the **Schema** that you can directly copy in the **Request Body JSON[1] Schema** text box:

```
{
    "properties":
    {    "humidity":
        {    "type": "integer"
        },
        "temperature":
        {    "type": "integer"
        }
    },
    "type": "object"
}
```

---

[1]The format of this is JSON (JavaScript Object Notation): a format commonly used to communicate data. JSON tends to be used more widely than csv files in IoT because it is very flexible and easy to extend/adapt.

Step 2: Passing Data into the ML Service

The next step in the workflow is to pass the temperature and humidity values to the Azure ML web service we set up in **Section 11.2**.

- In the designer view click **+ New step** (**Figure 11-19**).

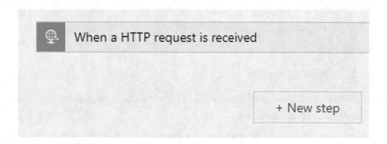

Figure 11-19. *Adding a new step*

- In the search box type **HTTP**. From the results select **HTTP** actions group (**Figure 11-20**).

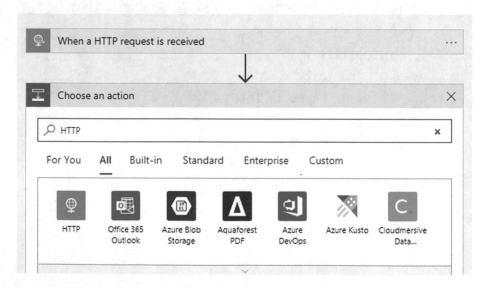

Figure 11-20. *Searching the "HTTP" actions group*

- This will expand to a few actions. From the **Actions** list, select **HTTP** action (**Figure 11-21**).

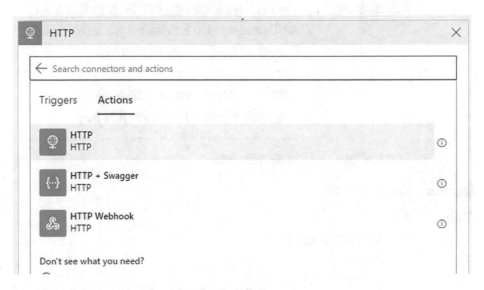

Figure 11-21. *Selecting the "HTTP" action*

- Provide the following information for the HTTP action:

Method:	POST
URI:	The Request URI copied from the "Request Response API Documentation for Weather prediction model [Predictive Exp.]". – See Section 11.5.

(continued)

Headers:	Accept	application/json
	Authorization	The API Key copied from the "Request Response API Documentation for Weather prediction model [Predictive Exp.]". – See Section 11.5.

> **Note**   Make sure to add a space between **Bearer** and the **API key**.

	Content-Type	application/json

Queries: Keep it as blank

BODY:
```
{
      "GlobalParameters": {},
      "Inputs": {
            "input1": {
                  "ColumnNames": [
                        "temperature",
                        "humidity"
                  ],
                  "Values": [
                        [
                              "value",
                              "value"
                        ]
                  ]
            }
      }
}
```

Cookie: Keep it as blank

Now in the **BODY**, replace the values for **temperature** and **humidity** with "**dynamic contents**".

- Highlight the first occurrence of the **"value"** (including the double quotes) and then select **temperature** from the **Dynamic content** pane (**Figure 11-22**).

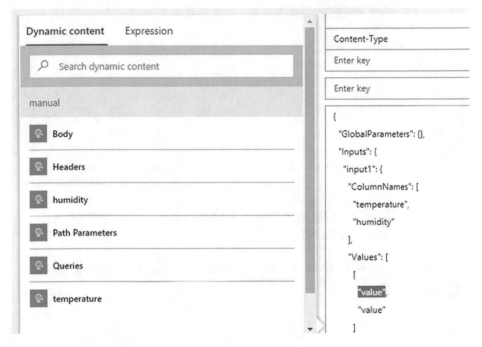

Figure 11-22. *Inserting dynamic content (step 1)*

- Next replace the second occurrence of the **"value"** with the dynamic content **"humidity"**.

Now your **JSON BODY** should look something like this (**Figure 11-23**).

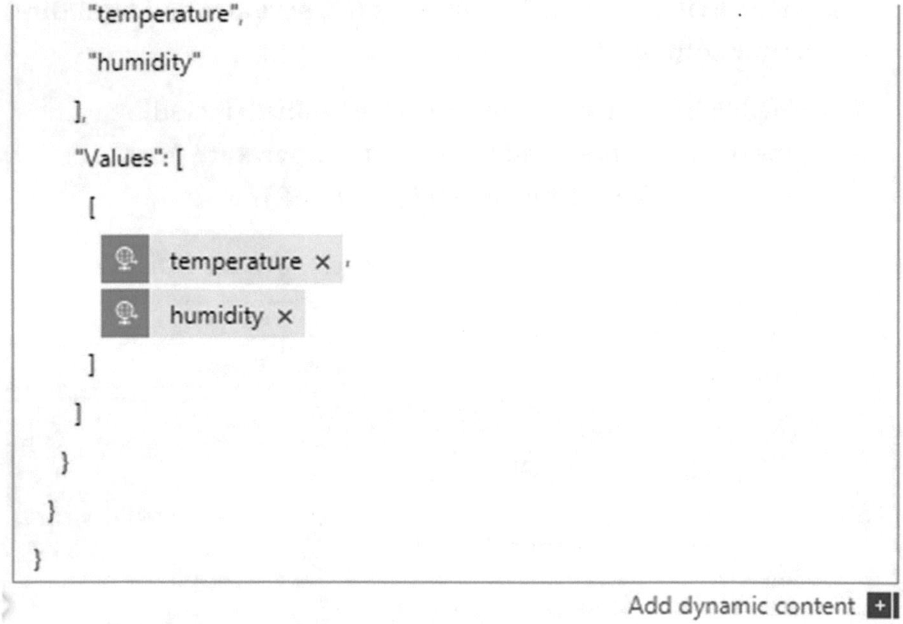

```
    "temperature",
    "humidity"
  ],
  "Values": [
    [
      🌐  temperature  ×
      🌐  humidity  ×
    ]
  ]
}
}
}
```

Add dynamic content ➕|

Figure 11-23. *Inserting dynamic contents (step 2). In this case, temperature and humidity*

Once completed the **HTTP** template should look something like this (**Figure 11-24**).

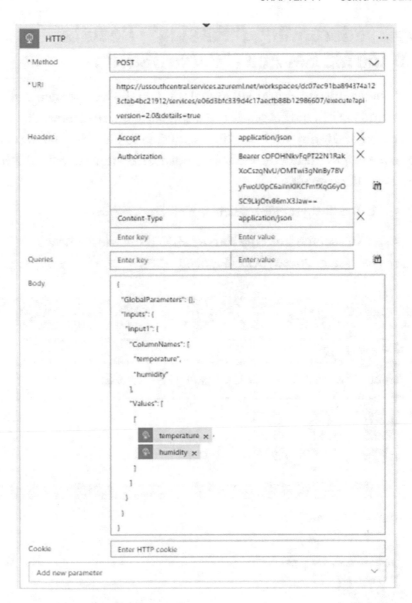

Figure 11-24. *"HTTP" action details*

Step 3: Interpreting ("Parsing") Results from the ML Service ("Parse JSON")

Data is passed into the Azure ML model through the web service as a **request** and the ML model sends the result back as a **response**. The response is a **JSON object** (i.e., a "file" with data in JSON format), and we need to parse it to extract the values we need. To do that we will add the action named **Parse JSON**.

- In the designer view select **+ New step**.

- In the search box type **Parse JSON**. From the **Actions** list, select **Parse JSON** (**Figure 11-25**).

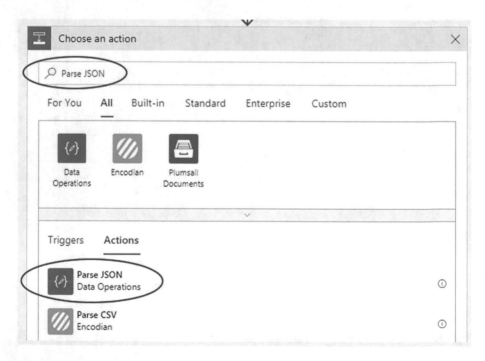

Figure 11-25. *Searching and selecting the "Parse JSON" action*

- Provide this information for the **Parse JSON** action as shown and described here:

Content: Click the Content box, and then from the Dynamic content, under HTTP, select Body.

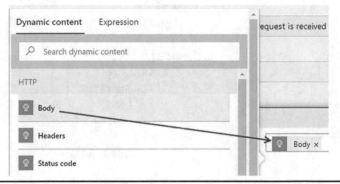

(continued)

Schema: {

```
            "properties": {
                "Results": {
                    "properties": {
                        "output1": {
                            "properties": {
                                "type": {
                                    "type": "string"
                                },
                                "value": {
                                    "properties": {
                                        "ColumnNames": {
                                            "items": {
                                                "type": "string"
                                            },
                                            "type": "array"
                                        },
                                        "ColumnTypes": {
                                            "items": {
                                                "type": "string"
                                            },
                                            "type": "array"
                                        },
                                        "Values": {
                                            "items": {
                                                "items": {},
                                                "type": "array"
                                            },
                                            "type": "array"
                                        }
                                    },
                                    "type": "object"
                                }
                            },
                            "type": "object"
                        }
                    },
                    "type": "object"
                }
            },
            "type": "object"
        }
```

Once completed the **Parse JSON** template should look something like this (**Figure 11-26**).

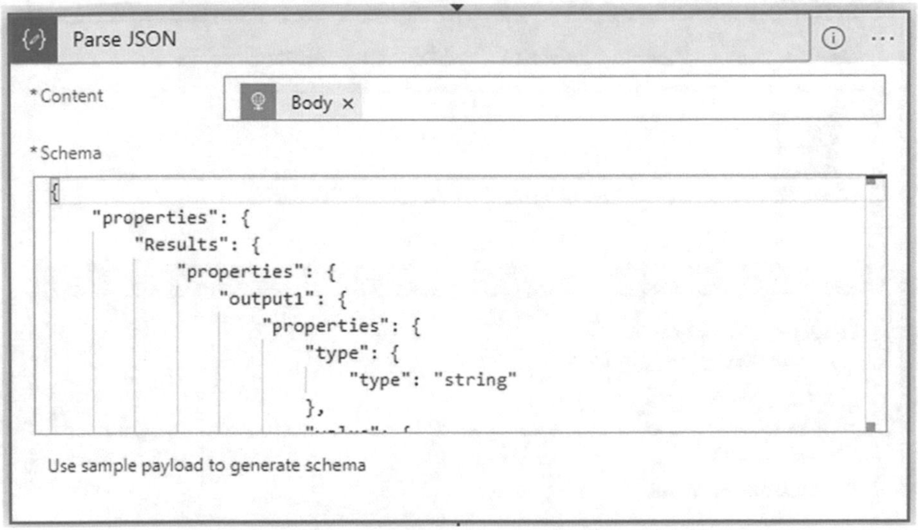

Figure 11-26. *"Parse JSON" action details*

Step 4: Setting Up a Variable to Store the Data from the ML Service

Now we need to assign the rain prediction score ("Yes" or "No") we are going to extract (parse) from the JSON object to a variable of type String. To do that we will add the action named **Initialize variable**.

- In the designer view select **+ New step**.

- In the search box type **Initialize variable**. From the **Actions** list, select **Initialize variable** (**Figure 11-27**).

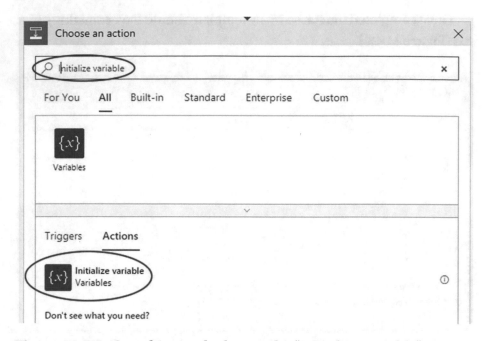

Figure 11-27. *Searching and selecting the "Initialize variable" action*

- Provide this information for the **Initialize variable**
  action as shown and described here:

Name: Score

Type: String

Value: We will use a formula to get the "Scored labels" in the two-dimensional
array:
body ('Parse_JSON')?['Results']?['output1']?['value']?['Values']?[0]?[2]

Once completed the **Initialize variable** template should look
something like this (**Figure 11-28**).

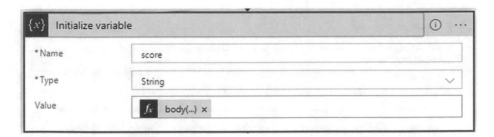

Figure 11-28. *"Initialize variable" action details*

Step 5: Sending Data Back to the Weather Station Instrument

Finally, we will send the variable **score** to the micro:bit to be displayed on the 5X5 LED matrix.

- In the designer view select **+ New step**.

- In the search box type **Response**. Wait for the search results. Then in the **Actions** list, select **Response** (**Figure 11-29**).

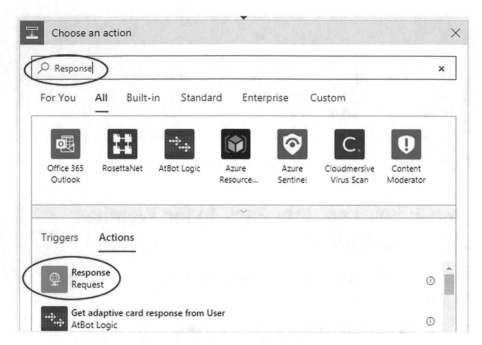

Figure 11-29. *Searching and selecting the "Response" action*

- Provide the information for the **Response** action shown here:

Status Code:	200
Headers:	Keep as blank
BODY:	Insert the dynamic variable **score** from the **Dynamic content** pane under the **Variables** category.

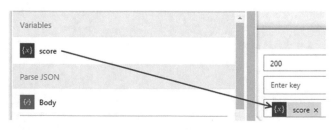

Once completed the **Response** template should look something like this (**Figure 11-30**).

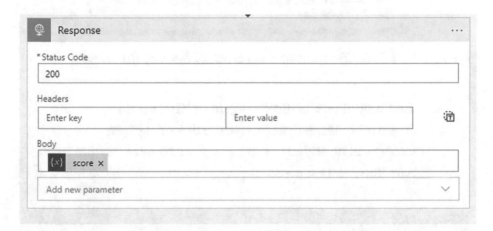

Figure 11-30. *"Response" action details*

We are done! Save your logic app: on the **designer** toolbar, click **Save**. This may take a few moments.

11.8 Testing the Workflow

Now we will start our logic app manually to test it:

- Run your logic app – on the **designer** toolbar, select **Run**. It may take a few moments to check your workflow. Once completed you will get a notification at the top-right corner of the page saying it has successfully checked the trigger of our logic app, and it should look something like this (**Figure 11-31**).

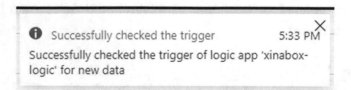

Figure 11-31. *Notification of a successful check of the trigger*

- Your workflow will display again in **RUN mode**
  (**Figure 11-32**). A tick icon (white tick on a green
  circle) will be added at the top-right corner of the title
  bars if the tests succeeded.

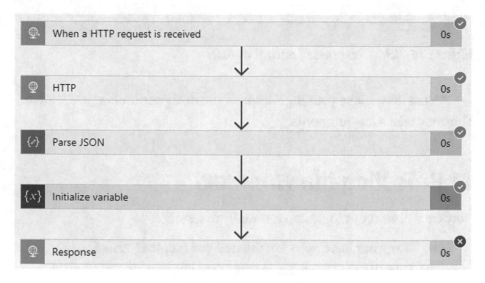

Figure 11-32. *Triggering the workflow manually*

- The **Response** action has a cross icon (cross on the
  gray background) on its title bar to indicate that the
  test was unsuccessful. To view the Response action's
  output details, click inside the Response action's
  title bar. You should see the message (**Figure 11-33**):

"ActionResponseSkipped". This is because the workflow did not receive any data from the hardware. That's OK for now: it will all work fine once we've hooked up the weather station.

Figure 11-33. *The response trigger displays the ActionResponse Skipped message*

- On the designer toolbar, select **Designer** to go back to the designer view.

We have now completed setting up and testing our IoT application, and our ML-powered predictive weather station is ready to go. We just need to start feeding data into it.

11.9 Summary

The process of using an ML service is very simple conceptually: you pass in some data, the ML service performs its black-box tricks, and a value is returned. It should not take scores of steps and endless options to set one up and use; but it does.

In this chapter we have set up and configured the IoT infrastructure needed to build our ML-powered predictive weather station. We have built an IoT application that includes an ML service: data from our digital instrument will be processed by the service and predictive data generated. This data is then sent back to our instrument and is displayed on a screen.

In the following chapter we will build the weather station digital instrument and hook it up to our IoT application.

CHAPTER 12

Connecting an Edge Device to the IoT Application

In the previous chapter we developed an IoT application that will ingest temperature and humidity data. This data will be processed by an ML service and a prediction will be made: is it likely to rain or not?

All that remains now is for us to build a device that can feed the required data into our IoT application and another device (or perhaps the same one) to receive the predictive data from the ML service and display it.

12.1 Choosing the Hardware

In this chapter we use the same hardware that we used in **Chapter 9**.

Throughout the book we have seen that when it comes to data science applications, the specific hardware instrument that we use is just an enabler: a means to an end. The outcomes – what the hardware enables – that is what is important, and any number of alternative hardware devices could have delivered the same outcomes.

This point is especially relevant here: we have just spent a long and arduous chapter building an IoT application and we will now spend a fraction of the time building an edge device. Once you have invested the

© Philip Meitiner, Pradeeka Seneviratne 2020
P. Meitiner and P. Seneviratne, *Beginning Data Science, IoT, and AI on Single Board Computers,*
https://doi.org/10.1007/978-1-4842-5766-1_12

time setting up your IoT application it is relatively trivial, by comparison at least. To switch out different edge devices.

A broad range of different edge devices could be used, including a mobile phone. If you can source temperature and humidity data on your phone, you could send it to the IoT application over Wi-Fi. Perhaps more likely is wanting to use a phone to receive the data: for example, trigger a text message whenever rain becomes likely. Hooking up a mobile phone is outside our scope here, but with the right tools it is similar to connecting a micro:bit.

One of the implications of this separation of the edge device and the IoT application is that the IoT application is effectively a stand-alone "product." It could be used by several different manufacturers of edge devices, competitors even. Consider a heart monitor that records someone's heart rate and uses AI to analyze the data. **Chapter 11** showed that building an AI-/ML-enabled IoT application that analyzes heart rate is unlikely to be trivial. An AI service that ingests this data and produces useful reports could be of great value to the health industry, especially to someone interested in building an edge device that might use the service.[1] IoT applications like the one we built are "assets" in and of themselves.

We will use the same hardware we have throughout: a micro:bit and weather sensor, with Wi-Fi capabilities added to provide IoT connectivity. The same components we used in **Chapter 9**.

---

[1] In the new covid19 world we find ourselves in, perhaps someone will build a machine learning system that is fed data from a bank of sensors that read a variety of personal health-related conditions (perhaps IR temperature, particulates, and C02 in exhaled breath, irregularity of heartbeat, frequency and pitch of coughing; there are so many different sensors available). The ML service would be trained to predict whether someone is infected with the virus, allowing us to identify the people most in need of early help.

12.2 The Role of the Edge Device

The edge device has two core functions:

- To measure and send weather data

- To receive and display predictive data

Figure 12-1 shows the role of the edge device (see **items 1** and **3**) as well as the linear process that our data will follow (it starts at 1, goes through 2, and then terminates at 3).

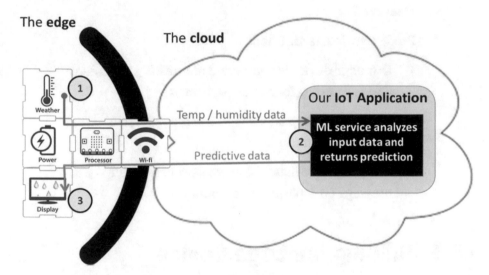

Figure 12-1. *The data flow from edge device to IoT application and back*

Referring to the numbers in **Figure 12-1**:

1. Data originates at our edge device:

    - Initially we need to connect to our IoT application.

    - We then need to measure temperature and humidity data.

    - This data is output to our IoT application using Wi-Fi.

2. Our IoT application follows its workflow, as per **Chapter 11**.

3. Predictive data is returned:

    - Our edge device is connected to our IoT application and is listening for messages from it.

    - When a message is received it is parsed into a format we can use.

    - The predictive data which we extract from the message is displayed on a screen.

12.3 Building the Edge Device

The instrument that we will use is identical to the one described in **Chapter 9**. **Figure 12-2** shows the hardware components; please refer to **Chapter 9** for more specifics. Connect the components you have at hand to build an instrument that approximates **Figure 12-2**.

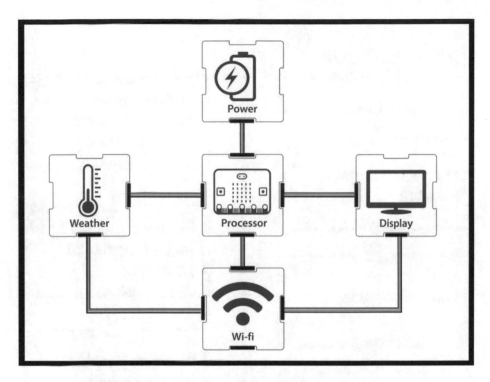

Figure 12-2. *Hardware components of our edge device*

12.4 Coding the Edge Device

The hardware instrument is little more than a paperweight, until we write the code we need to make it work the way we want it to. Before we start coding we need to understand exactly what it is we need the code to do.

Figure 12-3 presents the natural language code which we will convert into MakeCode blocks.

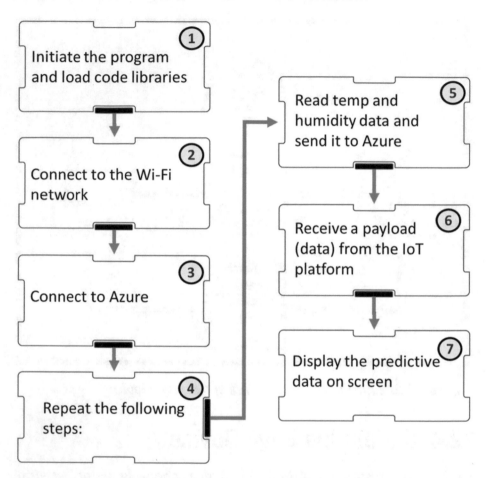

Figure 12-3. *Natural language code for the edge device*

No-code option: It is not possible to provide a no-code option for this tool – each program needs to be updated to include your Wi-Fi credentials and the Azure **HTTP Post URL**.

See **Section 12.7, "When a HTTP request is received,"** for details on how to find the **HTTP Post URL**.

A full version of the code is available on the supporting website for you to edit.

Table 12-1 shows how each step of the natural language code translates into MakeCode actions or blocks.

Table 12-1. *Developing code with MakeCode blocks*

Step	MakeCode
1	Start a new project.
	Add the XinaBox CW01 and SW01 extensions.
2	Add **CW01 connect to WiFi** block inside the **on start** block.
	Type in the SSID and password of your Wi-Fi network.

| 3 | Add the **CW01 connect to Azure with access endpoint** block. Then copy and paste the **HTTP POST URL**. |

	See **Section 12.7** for help in finding the **HTTP POST URL**.
	Make sure to delete the "https://" part from the **HTTP POST URL** when adding it to the block.
4	Add a **forever** block.

(continued)

Table 12-1. (*continued*)

Step	MakeCode
5, 6, and 7	Steps 5, 6, and 7 are all taken care of by a single block of code:

Add the **CW01 update two variables** block to the **forever** block.

Add the following in the four available spaces:

- **First variable**: Type in **"temperature"**.

- **Second variable**: Type in **"humidity"**.[2]

- **First value**: Add the **SW01 temperature (C)** block.

- **Second value**: Add the **SW01 humidity (%RH)** block.

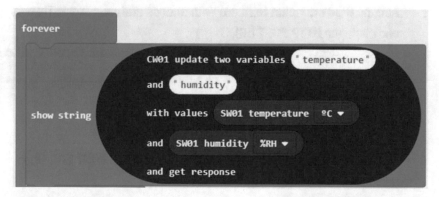

Finally, add a **pause** block. The delay should be at least long enough for the response to scroll on the screen.

---

[2]These are the same variable names that we saw in **Chapter 11** when we were setting up the IoT application. The names originated from the ML service we used, and throughout the process of setting up the IoT application, we did not need to enter them at all. There are a few places in the Azure workflow where you can view the variable names – for example, check **Chapter 11**, **Section 11.7**, Step 1. It is essential that you spell the variables correctly and use exactly the same case as is used in the IoT application.

Figure 12-4 shows the full code listing.

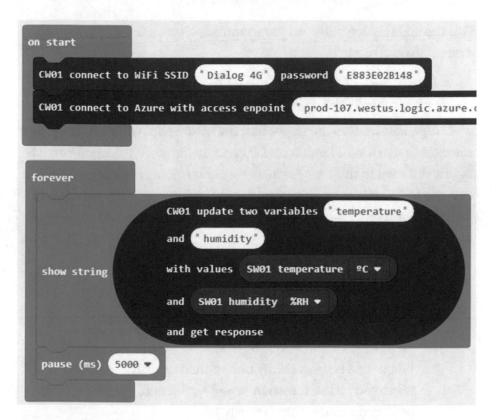

Figure 12-4. *MakeCode blocks for a micro:bit weather station*

When the code is complete, flash it onto your micro:bit and then remove the USB cable.

The function used earlier (**CW01 update two variables**...) is highly specialized: it was built specifically to integrate the BBC micro:bit with Azure ML services that take two variables as input and simultaneously return one variable as output.

The CW01 MakeCode extension also includes generic MQTT blocks (we used them in **Chapter 9**) that can be used to connect to any MQTT based IoT platform. We could not have used those blocks in this context: Azure is not easy to connect to from a micro:bit.

12.5 Using the Edge Device

With the edge device built and programmed, all we need to do now is power it up and use it.

*It is necessary to power up the weather station in a specific way, so please follow the steps described in **Chapter 9, Section 9.9**.*

Chapter 9 also lists the stages that the instrument will go through as it connects first to a Wi-Fi router and then to the targeted IoT platform. It is slightly different in this case because we are receiving and displaying data from the IoT platform too. If the process is working correctly you should see the following:

1. If the instrument has connected to the Wi-Fi network the letter C will display on the micro:bit LED screen.

2. The micro:bit will then try to connect to Azure and start to send data to our IoT application.

3. When data is successfully transmitted a tick is displayed on the screen followed by the rain prediction result ("Yes" or "No").

The weather station will continue to share and display this data until you turn it off.

When you first see the "Yes" or "No" scrolling on the micro:bit LEDs, you are entitled to feel a great deal of satisfaction: you have achieved something that even a few years ago would not have been possible. The weather prediction application is the (unofficial) Hello World! of ML, and **Chapter 13** will elaborate on what other, more complex, applications this simple ML experiment unlocks for us.

12.6 Improving the Edge Device

The edge device is as simple as can be: the barest minimum of code and hardware was used – just five hardware modules and six blocks of code.

We could enhance the instrument either by adding more components or by making the code more sophisticated. Using techniques we've covered in this book you should be able to implement some of the following enhancements:

- Add a decent display and print data to it.

- When the A button is clicked, show the status of the connection.

- Process the prediction data – do something when the prediction is "Yes" and something else when it is "No" – why not show a graphic to indicate rain?

- Control the frequency with which data is sent and received or only send when the B button is clicked.

- Do you have credentials for more than one Wi-Fi network? Use constant variables and try to auto-connect to whichever is in range.

12.7 Peering Under the Hood of the IoT Application

Looking at our micro:bit screen scrolling the word "Yes" or "No" and then looking out the window to check if it's raining... that is only fun for so long. When you get bored of it, pop back to the IoT application, while the edge device is still active, and take a look at what is going on in there.

Open the **Azure logic app designer** and click **Run** on the designer toolbar to run data through your workflow. It may take a few moments for things to load up, after which the workflow will be displayed. You should recognize the five steps listed in **Figure 12-5** from **Chapter 11**.

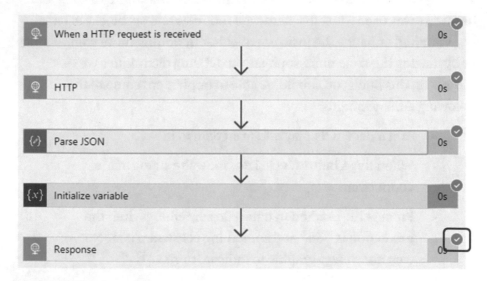

Figure 12-5. Manually triggered workflow: the green tick on the Response tab shows it is in RUN mode

If the edge device is still working you should have opened the workflow in **RUN** mode: if it has loaded properly you will see a tick icon (white tick on a green circle) added to the title bar of the **Response** action. This indicates that your logic app has received confirmation that the data transaction between Azure and the micro:bit has been successfully completed. From here we can look into each stage of the workflow to see what is going on and check the live data that it is being handled.

Tip If you still get a "**cross**" icon on the **Response** action's title bar, make sure the edge device is functioning properly and then run the logic app again, and again, until you get the "**tick**".

We will look at a few elements of the workflow.

Parse JSON

When we created the workflow, our Parse JSON file was set up for us and contained variable names, not values. Now that data is being passed through the workflow, we can see what the JSON file looks like with live content:

- Click the **Parse JSON** action.

- Scroll down and find the section **OUTPUTS**.

- Click the body and scroll down the text box.

Figure 12-6 shows the parsed array containing the temperature and humidity values from the micro:bit, as well as the rain prediction results from the ML service.

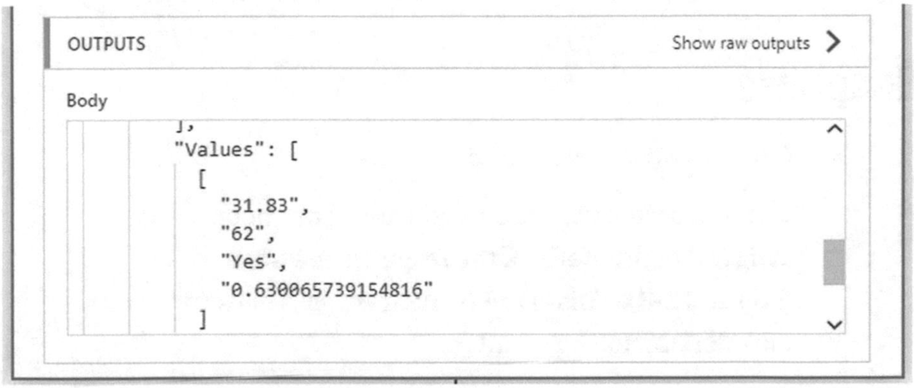

Figure 12-6. *The output of the Parse JSON action*

Initialize Variable

- Click the **Initialize variable** action.

When the workflow was originally set up, a variable called **score** was created. This is the variable that stores our prediction: it is a String that contains either "Yes" or "No".

Figure 12-7 shows that the result in score is currently **Yes**.

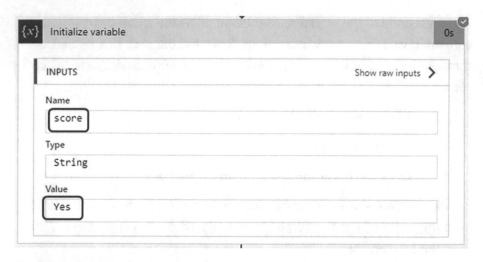

Figure 12-7. *The output of the Initialize variable action*

Response

- Click the **Response** action.

    The **score** variable (discussed earlier) has been
    assigned to the **Body** of the response message
    (**Figure 12-8**). This is the content we pass back to
    the micro:bit as the result.

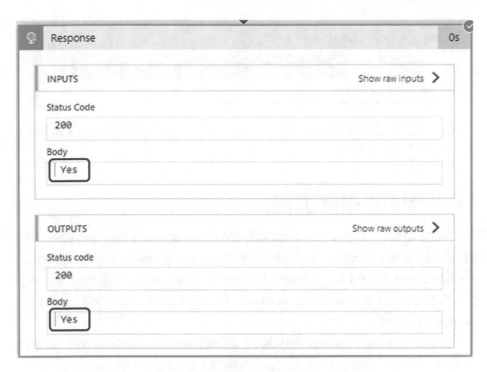

Figure 12-8. *The output of the Response action*

When a HTTP Request Is Received

- Click the **When a HTTP request is received** action.

This information does not change during running of the workflow; the **HTTP POST URL** can be found here (Figure 12-9). This parameter is crucial as it is used in the MakeCode block **CW01 connect to Azure with access endpoint** to connect to the Azure-based IoT application.

Figure 12-9. *The When a HTTP request is received action showing the HTTP POST URL*

12.8 Data Analysis

It is normal at this stage of a data science experiment to begin to analyze the data we have collected. But hasn't that already been done by the ML service when it used the temperature and humidity data to produce our prediction? Has our role been subverted: are we now redundant in the analysis phase?

The answer is a resounding NO! As with most areas of the data science process, where automation occurs it frees us from tasks that are repetitive and laborious and allows us to use our not-artificial intelligence to focus on things that cannot be automated.

In this instance our analytical gaze falls on the results: How intelligent or useful are they? What could we do with the results to extract value from them? Are there any ethical considerations? We should not just accept the results at face value: our role is to question them and check whether they are logical, believable, and useful. We should ask whether artificial intelligence is really driving the analysis, or is it just a sophisticated algorithm?

Why not record the results from the ML service over an extended period and add your own data (whether it is raining or not). Then use the analysis techniques to see just how effective the predictions really are. How strongly do the predictions made by the ML service correlate with it actually raining?

While these questions, and their answers, will have a bearing on how much faith we put in our weather prediction data, the efficacy of that prediction is only of secondary importance to what we have achieved in this chapter. Using one ML service means being able to use many, as we will discuss in **Chapter 13**.

What may cause some readers concern is the absence of any obvious way in which the ML service can learn: if we are not providing feedback on the accuracy of the predictions, then how does the service know whether its predictions are accurate and how can it learn from its mistakes?

The element that is missing from our IoT application is **training**. When an ML service is first set up, it undergoes a period of training, where a human operator provides information about the accuracy of the results it is generating.

A simple example is an ML service that can distinguish between an image of a cat and a dog. When the ML service is initially set up, a person will provide it with images that are identified as "cat" or "dog". The ML will extrapolate visual features that correlate with "cat" or "dog" and will begin to classify new images that are provided. As the ML begins to distinguish cats and dogs, the role of the person is to train the ML by reviewing the results and identifying correct/incorrect ones. The ML will continue to adapt until the person accepts the accuracy of the model and stops training it.

We have not focused on training here: our goal in this book was to use an ML service for data science work, not to learn how build/set up a machine learning service or help to make it more accurate. Training an ML service is interesting and helps provide an intuitive understanding of how it works, but a consumer ML service does not need to include a training element.[3] When we, as consumers, use an email service, we do not expect to have to train it in how to send emails. In the same way, there is a demand for fully formed ML services (like the one we used) to be available to non-expert consumers. The process of building an ML service, including training it, is something that in the future a significant proportion of the people who use ML services will know very little about.

12.9 Summary

We have almost come to the end of our data science journey and, in the process, we have looked at a broad range of technologies and techniques, all of them in some way useful to us in our data science endeavors.

It is quite normal for developers to build up a personal library of modules/functions that they reuse extensively: their toolkit. As a programmer masters a new concept, they develop code fragments/functions that help them exploit it. Years later they might have forgotten aspects of the concept, but they will still know exactly how to use their functions.

---

[3]If a consumer ML service allows members of the public to train it, then there is a risk that people will mistrain it, either by accident or willfully. Sometimes getting the public to train an ML is a good idea:

- Google's Captcha software purportedly identified humans from bots trying to access a website. The responses we have all provided when using Captcha are used to train Google's ML image recognition software.

It has also been known to backfire:

- In 2016 Microsoft released a chatbot called Tay on twitter. Tay was set up to learn from conversations. Within a day Tay had developed a nasty streak that resulted in Microsoft having to suspend its account. This was an example of willful mistraining of an AI and shows that caution should be exercised when training an ML service.

You should regard the different techniques that you have succeeded in implementing throughout this book as part of your toolkit; in building the edge device in this chapter we have done very little new (besides using a few new blocks in MakeCode): we combined stuff that we had already developed. The point made early on about the value of modularity and reusability has been implicitly proven by the ease with which we were able to build the required instrument.

Your toolkit has now reached a point where it has critical mass: the potential to be used for a broad variety of novel and unexpected applications. In the next and final chapter we will look at ways in which the toolkit that we have built up throughout this book can be useful to you once you've put the book down.

CHAPTER 13

Consolidating our Learnings

In this, the final chapter, we will review what we have covered in this book and look at how the skills we've learned can be used in different contexts. With the journey all but over, what does the destination look like and where might we go from here? What else can we use our data science toolkit for?

13.1 Am I a Data Scientist?

Congratulations on making it this far. If you've followed the chapters, worked through the examples and everything has made sense, then you have a solid foundation in data science and the ability to apply it in real-world situations.

Of course, just like studying the basics of biology does not make one a doctor, so having a solid foundation in data science does not make one a data scientist. The information and techniques outlined in this book are a stepping-stone: useful in and of themselves and potentially the first step toward becoming a professional data scientist. But what is a "professional data scientist"?

Doctors, nurses, architects, plumbers: disciplines like these require accreditation before the title can be rightfully used. That involves studying a prescribed body of knowledge and passing through some or other

© Philip Meitiner, Pradeeka Seneviratne 2020
P. Meitiner and P. Seneviratne, *Beginning Data Science, IoT, and AI on Single Board Computers*,
https://doi.org/10.1007/978-1-4842-5766-1_13

qualification process. There is no universally accepted data scientist accreditation, no governing body, and no final exam: anyone can call themselves a data scientist.

As to the question of whether you are a data scientist: in your job or day-to-day life do you work with data, process and analyze that data, interpret it and produce actionable output? If so, then maybe you are.

13.2 Becoming a Data Scientist

While the loose/informal definition of what makes someone a data scientist is interesting, when companies are hiring data scientists they generally have a clear idea of what they are looking for. This tends to be a set of skills/experiences that relate to how the company already undertakes data science, and it is very common to see jobs advertised requiring specific skills such as coding (e.g., in Python), SQL, statistics and machine learning.

If you are interested in exploring data science further, potentially making a living from it, there are many disciplines to study and a huge range of directions to go in. One of the best ways to get an understanding of what skills matter in the field of data science is to look at job boards.

Most of the skills required can be learned, and if you've found that you are comfortable with the material in the book then you probably have the aptitude required to do so. One theme has been consistent throughout this journey, and that is the role that curiosity plays in the process. The skills mentioned are valuable, but what makes a great data scientist is their curiosity, their drive to ask questions. Intuition is also highly prized: being curious about the right things and being able to ask the right questions are traits that computers are nowhere near able to replicate. And remember, you don't need to be able to think like a computer: we have computers to do that for us.

13.3 Debunking Some Myths

From a data science point of view, myths are hypotheses/facts that have been accepted by people to be true/proven, but which are not based on any reliable or verifiable data.[1] It is somewhat ironic that a field like data science has its own set of myths. The problem with myths are that they often look like barriers to people on the other side, so we'll take a look at a few and try to debunk them:

Only data scientists do real data science.

- **Data science** is what we have been doing throughout this book – using scientific methods to gather, process, and perform all manner of operations on data.

- Until a professional standard is established, a **data scientist** is someone who is employed in a job with "Data Scientist" in the title. The term is used professionally to refer to the analytical aspects of the process. The team member who builds and codes the sensor arrays would not be called the data scientist. But they are participating in data science: it is a team operation, and the data scientist is a member of that team.

Real data scientists do not use Excel/spreadsheets.

- A novice uses Excel excessively.

- An expert never uses Excel.

- A guru uses Excel when it is appropriate.

---

[1]Myths that are found to be true cease to be myths and become facts, of course.

You have to be a strong coder to be a data scientist.

- Data scientists will find themselves in situations where coding is required. It is a great skill to have.

- But when some code needs to be written, a data scientist can use a developer to write it for them.

- The key is knowing what to ask the developer for: what are the outcomes needed from the code? Any good developer should have no problem converting well thought-out natural language code into real code.

Only big corporations and universities can afford it.

- It is possible for a single individual on a budget to undertake real, affordable and novel data science experimentation.

- Given the sheer volume of data that is being generated daily, and with so much of it being free and easy to access online, how many fascinating, groundbreaking and useful correlations are there waiting to be found, perhaps only a few clicks away?

You have to be exceptionally intelligent to be a data scientist.

- Data science is an intellectual field, but anyone with the right curiosity and drive can learn the techniques needed.

- Of course highly intelligent people tend to do well in a range of intellectual fields, including data science.

Market research is not real data science.

- Especially in academia, market research is looked down on as being substandard; some might say it is guilty of "selling out" – putting profit before quality.

- There is good and bad market research just like there is good and bad academic research.

- The real difference is that we so often see bad market research splashed on billboards and thrust in our faces on advertising. This does not represent the full range and potential of the market research industry.

- An example of nontrivial market research in post-apartheid South Africa will help illustrate a more positive application.

Back in the 1990s, advisers to the ANC used a small market research company based in Durban (the now defunct Research Surveys) who had an innovative product called "The Conversion Model". This was a survey technique which was surprisingly effective at measuring predicted behavioral responses from different groups of people to specific messages. In a nutshell, would this message incite or unite?

Mr. Mandela was without question one of the greatest statesmen of his, or any, era, and while the ANC were assured of victory in the national elections it was a priority of his to ensure that all the different race groups in the country were engaged with, and excited by, the process of transforming South Africa into the Rainbow Nation.

Multiple conversion model surveys were commissioned to assess which parts of the ANC's message resonated the best with different race groups and which ones were most polarizing. Mr. Mandela's government of national unity did a great job of prioritizing items that helped keep a broad spectrum of the population enthused and optimistic.

13.4 Extrapolating Learnings

With access to the right hardware there is no limit to the range and sophistication of digital instruments that you can build using the techniques outlined in this book. Most of the skills we have covered are transferrable:

If you can connect one sensor to a microprocessor:

- Whatever peripheral system you are using (XinaBox, breadboards, SparkFun, etc.), if you have successfully connected one sensor to a microprocessor, then you can usually apply the same method to attach other sensors too. If you choose a peripheral system with a broad range of sensors, you should be able to attach any of these.

- As long as the microprocessor supports it (and most do), you can connect several sensors at the same time and build instruments capable of measuring a broad range of sensor readings.

- And remember, in 2020+ you do not need an engineering degree or a soldering iron to build high-quality and robust digital instruments.

- **Figure 13-1** shows two digital instruments built with xChips. We built the Wi-Fi gateway shown on the left, while the device shown on the right could be used in a high-altitude balloon to record and transmit environmental data.

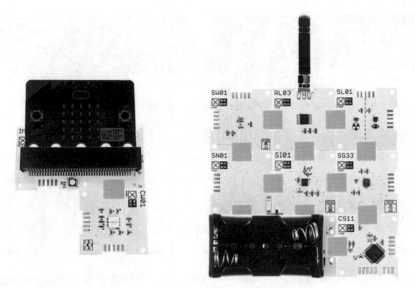

Figure 13-1. *Two digital instruments of differently complexity built using the same principles*

If you can write block code for micro:bit:

- Then you **can** write code: you can program.

- There are a LOT of microprocessors that can take block code. And most of them are orders of magnitude more powerful than the micro:bit. You **can** program these too, using the same techniques.

- **Figure 13-2** shows the Maker.Makecode block coding environment. This is a Microsoft product – the micro:bit MakeCode we used is a "white label" implementation of this block coding environment.

- The interface, syntax, flashing process are very similar – they will be familiar to users of MakeCode.

- **Figure 13-2** shows a selection of the boards that can be coded using block code.

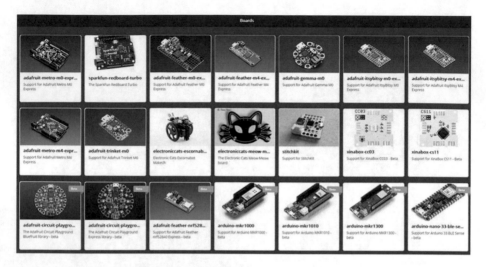

Figure 13-2. *A selection of boards that can be programmed using block code in Microsoft's Maker.Makecode*

If you can program a microprocessor to read data from a sensor:

- Then you can program it to read data from any sensor. You know how to load libraries/extensions, and the blocks to read sensor data tend to work in a very similar way. Finding the right extension for a specific sensor can be the trickiest part: look for manufacturers who provide easy-to-use (and find) MakeCode extensions for the microprocessor you are using.

- Reading data from more than one sensor is trivial: you should be able to read from an array of many sensors simultaneously.

- **Figure 13-3** shows four MakeCode extensions for different types of sensor. The names of the variables change, but in each case the value from the sensor is returned as a simple variable, a number. The paradigm is the same.

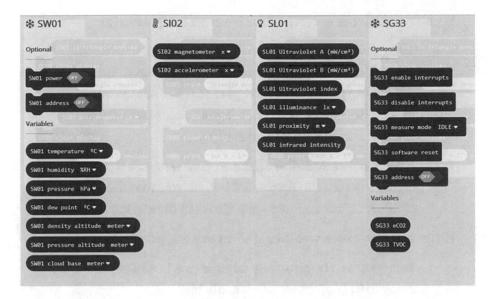

Figure 13-3. *Four MakeCode extensions for four different sensors*

If you can analyze temperature and humidity data:

- Then you can analyze any two data sets using the same techniques.

- You should be able to extend this: add other data sets, experiment with different types of visualizations, hunt for correlations, and add trend lines.

If you can connect to an IoT platform:

- Then you can send and receive data from an online platform and access services on the cloud.

- The power of the online platform and the services available can be used to add sophistication to your digital instrument.

If you can process received data from an IoT platform:

- Then you can use/respond to commands or data from that IoT platform. These commands/data have had the processing power of the IoT platform behind them: processing power orders of magnitude greater than is available on the SBC you are using.

- If you can get an IoT platform to send data to a remote digital instrument, then an AI/ML service that the IoT platform is hooked up to can also sent data to it.

If you can hook up a weather station to a ML predictive model:

- Then you can hook up any edge device to any of the many ML predictive models available.

As recently as 20, maybe even 10 years ago, a comparable set of skills would have taken a bright and motivated individual many years to acquire. But with modern technology it is possible to gain those skills more quickly and focus on how to apply them, on the things that the technology can enable, rather than fiddling with the technology itself. Data science is a layer on top of digital technology, and being able to delve into it like we have done here is a luxury that would not have been possible until quite recently: within the lifetime of most readers.

13.5 Applying Our Knowledge to Different Builds

Using the skills outlined in the previous section you could build all sorts of things, such as

- An instrument with an array of sensors that connects to an IoT platform

- And that sends data which is then passed into an ML model

- The ML generates predictions or key metrics which are sent back (perhaps to a completely different device/devices)

- And where a series of real-world electronic switches or motors are turned on/off

- All this time information is output on one or more screens, perhaps on devices in different locations

- And is written to a file and backed up on the IoT platform

While this might sound complex, it is extremely generic: the core architecture of any number of modern inventions/gadgets. With this basic model, you can build a huge range of things, including:

- A tool to monitor the air quality of a classroom, or bedroom, or airport waiting room. Data is collected by sensors in the room and shared by Wi-Fi with an ML service, which analyzes the data and remotely controls a window, blinds, fan, dehumidifier, and air conditioner as appropriate to maintain a healthy environment at minimal energy cost.

- Having trouble sleeping? Build a sensor array to monitor factors in your bedroom. Collect a few weeks' worth of sensor data and add in data about how well you slept. Identify sensor readings that correlate with you sleeping well; then build an instrument that can manage the relevant factors to give you an optimal environment.

- What about a chess playing robot? Or a robot that can sort different colored jelly beans? Or one that can pick ripe strawberries?

- Building and maintaining a controlled environment such as an enclosure for an "exotic" pet.

- Cities like London have large flood gates which are closed when water levels get too high. But it takes time to close them, and it is often costly to do so. A range of sensor arrays upstream and weather report data all being fed into an ML model which predicts flooding could make for a very efficient control system.

- There are rural villages in India that are visited by wild roaming elephants who are known to eat crops and cause damage. A series of arrays and actuators spread around a village might be capable of setting off loud noises or lights to divert elephants away.

13.6 Ethical Considerations

So, you can now undertake all manner of experimentation and build all sorts of innovative and potentially impactful contraptions. But what kind of things shouldn't you build?

Obviously nothing that risks causing physical injury or criminal damage: we know a line exists. So, if there is a line between what is OK and what isn't, then where is that line?

To find the answer, we need to look into ethics:

What is/are "ethics"? Many people would agree that at the core of most ethical arguments is the tenet that if you are engaged in any activity that impacts on other people then you have some kind of responsibility for any effect this activity has on those people. Ethics shines a light on that responsibility.

Data science is used to inform decisions and policies that touch our lives in a wide range of different ways, as we have seen throughout this book. Is ethical consideration necessary though?

Data science can appear to be scientific, unbiased, and impartial: the methods and tools are independent of the data that is being analyzed. The same techniques used to analyze temperature and humidity data would work for religious affiliation and IQ data: a correlation coefficient does not have an opinion.

A study into religious affiliation and IQ data is without doubt going to arouse passion, anger, and hurt and could very easily be manipulated (e.g., different IQ tests have cultural biases). Whether it would be ethical or not to actually gather and study this data is not a judgment we will make here. At the point of conception of an idea, the impact of implementing that idea should be considered though; you are your own ethical guardian.

The field of ethics is fascinating and vast, but we have almost run out of space. The important point to make here is that data science is not exempt: good people can produce bad science.

Most important is to remember that, with the growth of AI and ML, the human component of data science may change or even shrink. But it is humans who create the need for ethical considerations and who need to be the guardians of ethics. The best AI/ML cannot come near to a human in terms of empathy and passion for the value of ethics. As we hand over aspects of the data science process to AI/ML, we need to cling to ownership of this key consideration.

So, before we conclude, an ethical dilemma to ponder:

Is it OK to scare off elephants who are just foraging, and what is the impact on the elephants? Will everyone who answers this question have the same answer? Do the opinions of people whose lives are not affected by the elephants matter? What happens if we extend the metaphor and substitute elephants with groups of migrant people?

13.7 Summary

The original plan for this final summary was to list all the bits and bobs that have been featured in the book: make you feel good about attaining a very useful and practical body of skills and techniques.

Instead the authors would like to completely break the fourth wall and end on a somewhat less conventional note:

Hi. Thank you for investing your time and money in this book.

We started writing back in August 2019, in the pre-covid19 world, and we are finishing it in April 2020. So much has changed since then, and we share your loss and sadness.

We still want to end on an upbeat note though.

This crisis will pass and those that remain will emerge stronger from it. When the war on Coronavirus is finally won, society must, and will, remember the heroes who got us through it: the nurses, doctors, orderlies, truck drivers, shelf stackers, teachers, police, farmers, shopkeepers… the list goes on.

And it includes data scientists, front and center.

During the height of this crisis it is hard to look at a screen and not see a chart showing infection/survival rates, or hear experts talk about models projecting predicted outcomes, or read about the expected impact on the global economy. Data science is at the heart of all of these endeavors, informing the life-or-death decisions that governments are being forced to make on a daily, even hourly, basis. The strategy and implementation of self-isolation is based on data science modeling and the development and testing of new medicines will use data science techniques. Next to medicine, data science might be the best weapon we have in our arsenal.

We will leave you with this final thought: what we have looked at in this book is small and frivolous in comparison to the work described earlier, but our efforts share the same DNA as these endeavors. The great scientists who are leading us through this crisis were once at the same stage of their data science journey as you are now.

Thank you and stay safe.

Index

A

Analog and digital
    thermometer, 33–34
Analysis tools
  average, 36
  correlation (*see* Correlation
    coefficients)
  data quality, 36
  experimental design, 105
  extremities, 35
  introspection, 36–37
  key statistical functions, 119–121
  maximum and minimum
    values, 35
  reporting data, 122–123
  software, 106–107
  spreadsheet program, 107–108
  statistical significance, 123–125
  visualization tools, 120–121
ArduinoIDE/mBed, 153
Artificial intelligence (AI/ML)
  data analysis, 226
    charts representation, 229
    correlations, 227–228
    dataset labels, 227
    human intelligence, 230
    temperature data, 228

data science working, 215–217
definition, 212–214
environmental factors, 218–220
hardware
  data logging, 223
  requirements, 221–222
  snapshots, 224–225
  tagged data collection, 226
vs. human, 231–233
intelligent behaviors, 213–214
IQ test method, 212–213
Kasparov, Gary, 216
key differences, 214
software, 223–224
Atmospheric (air) pressure, 52
Azure logic apps
  basics tab details, 252–253
  deployment confirmation
    message, 253–254
  resource selection, 252
  steps, 251

B

Bluetooth, 137
  BLE (*see* Bluetooth Low
    Energy (BLE))
  components, 142